# STORIES THAT BIND

VARIETY CROSSING 10TH VOLUME

KCLF-21
PRESS

Variety Crossing 10th Volume


National Library of Canada Cataloguing in Publication Data

Variety Crossing
ISSN 1706-9025
ISBN 978-0-9782020-8-8 (10th Volume)

1. Canadian poetry (Korean)--Periodicals.
2. Canadian poetry--20th century--Periodicals.
3. Canadian poetry--21st century--Periodicals.
4. Canadian literature (Korean)--Periodicals.
5. Canadian literature--20th century--Periodicals.
6. Canadian literature--21st century--Periodicals.
I. Korean-Canadian Literary Forum-21

PS8001.V37 C895.7'1008
C2003-300580-X

Publisher: Dae-Tong Huh
Editor: Dae-Tong Huh
Coeditor: Eugene Huh
Design & Layout: Eugene Huh
Cover Design: Eugene Huh

Korean-Canadian Literary Forum-21
PO BOX 45035
5854 Yonge St.
Willowdale, ON M2M 4K3 Canada
Phone & Fax: 416-222-7935
E-mail: dt_huh@yahoo.ca and varietycrossing@gmail.com
Web site: www.varietycrossing.org

The Korean-Canadian Literary Forum-21 Press acknowledges support from

ONTARIO ARTS COUNCIL
CONSEIL DES ARTS DE L'ONTARIO

*Printed and bound in Canada*

# STORIES THAT BIND

VARIETY CROSSING 10TH VOLUME

*10th Anniversary Special Anthology*

*As the river of stars brightens the night sky,*

*let this world, too, become bright with stars of hope.*

*Let us welcome peace and cherish hope using our pens*

*and our collective wisdom.*

# Acknowledgements

*We gratefully acknowledge*
*Dalton McGuinty, David Macfarlane, Joe Fiorito,*
*George Elliott Clarke, Nicole Brossard, Barry Callaghan, Anne Michaels,*
*Priscila Uppal, Ko Un, Yevgeny Yevtushenko, Hyo-Chee Moon, Suji Kwock Kim,*
*Brian McKenna, Robert Dickson, Joe Rosenblatt & Catherine Owen, Sonnet L' Abbe,*
*Robert Sward, Nham Cho Kim, Gil-Won Lee,Paul Saltzman, Lien Chao, Dae-Tong Huh,*
*Flavia Cosma,Je-Chun Park, Kyung-Whan Yoo, Kijo Song, Flavia Cosma, George Fethering,*
*Mikhail Park, Hae-Myung Byun, Patria Rivera, Ben Viccari, Antonio D'Alfonsor,*
*Harry J. Huang, Ashok Bhargava, Charles Siedlecki,*
*and our members and associates*
*for their permission to reproduce their poems in this volume.*

# CONTENTS

## Welcome

## Poetry

## Essay

## Short Story

## Non-Fiction



## Interview



## Biography

# Welcome

Ontario

Premier of Ontario – Premier ministre de l'Ontario

November 21 – 23, 2008

## A PERSONAL MESSAGE FROM THE PREMIER

On behalf of the Government of Ontario, I am delighted to extend warm greetings to everyone attending Stories that Bind: An International Festival and Conference, hosted by the Korean Canadian Literary Forum-21 Press.

Ontario's and Canada's strength comes from the diversity and knowledge of its people. *Variety Crossing* is a multicultural collection of poetry, essays and writings by Canadians of all backgrounds. My colleagues and I appreciate the significant role the anthology plays in enabling diverse voices from across the country to be heard.

I would like to take this opportunity to congratulate the Korean Canadian Literary Forum-21 Press on marking its 10th anniversary. To all those involved with this fine organization — I applaud your fine efforts in promoting creative expression. Well done!

Please accept my best wishes for a highly successful festival — and much ongoing success.

**Dalton McGuinty**
**Premier**

# 온타리오 주지사의 친서

본인은 온타리오 주정부를 대신하여 한카문학출판사가 주체하는 한데 묶은 스토리 행사: 국제적인 축제와 컨퍼런스에 참석하신 모든 분들에게 뜨거운 환영의 뜻을 표하는 바입니다.

온타리오주와 캐나다의 장점은 다양성에 있으며 다양한 시민들의 지식에 기인 된다고 봅니다. 버라이어티(복합문예집)는 배경이 서로 다른 캐나다 문인들의 작품 시, 수필, 복합문학작품을 모아 담고 있습니다. 나의 동료들과 본인은 이 문예지가 캐나다 전역에 특별한 다양성의 역할을 선물하고 있음에 그 가치를 높이 평가하는 바입니다.

본인은 이 기회를 빌어 한카문학출판사의 10주년 출판기념에 축하를 보냅니다. 한카문학 비영리출판사에 연루한 모든 분들의- 성공적이고 창의적인 노력에 본인은 아낌없는 갈채를 보냅니다.
놀라운 성취입니다!

훌륭하고 성공적인 축제가 되길 바라며—아울러 이런 축제가 계속해서 대성공 하길 바랍니다.

달톤 맥퀸티
온타리오 주수상

*Translated by Dae-Tong Huh.*

# Preface

## Culture and Literature Among Neighbours Without Walls

By Dae-Tong Huh
President of KCLF-21 Press

I was born in Korea in 1937, a few years before Korea had been liberated from the Japanese occupation in 1945. Although it was an important event in my country's history, it was a terrible time around the world, with millions and millions killed during the World War.

By the time I was twelve years old, I had lost my loving father and grandfather because of war – both the World War as well as the fratricidal war between The South and The North of Korea. It was on June 25, 1950, that my country began a blood battle, much like Germany has also experienced. The difference is that the conflict in my country is still ongoing, where it is known as the Unfinished War.

Conflict is never easy. Between individuals, it can be managed. But as we have seen from events in Vietnam, Iraq and Afghanistan now, conflict between nations, races or between faiths is devastating.

This international festival and conference is a source of the world's most powerful communication and understanding for the future to defeat conflict. Of course, I don't mean missiles, hydrogen bombs, or even atomic bombs. I mean the powerful spirit of literature and the ideas that writers can convey. The message of peace from a poet's heart is a far more effective weapon than a bullet.

In the valleys of Korea, where my footsteps still echo, my life was influenced by the language, the culture and the literature of my heritage. It strikes me every day how wonderful it is to be Korean. My hope is that you feel the same about your background, because it is your language, both spoken and written, that makes your culture valuable to the rest of us.

Although in my heart I am Korean, I have lived in Canada for over 40 years. I am a Canadian citizen, and in this country I am allowed to be known as a Korean-Canadian. Canada has opened its arms to the world as a country where diversity is embraced. Different races, different languages and different cultures are encouraged to live together. In Canada, we enjoy a true multicultural society, where the mosaic is preferred over the melting pot.

Our closest neighbours, the US, have often been referred to as this melting pot or salad bowl, where cultures are expected to come together as one flavour.

On the other hand, Canada's society was built upon the base of the Aboriginals, rather than trying to tear it down. As each wave of immigrants arrived, we built on what was there already, expanding instead of shrinking. This blend grew to the point of having Canada officially adopt a multicultural policy in 1971, becoming the first country in the world whose government actually acknowledged the importance of diversity. Cultural diversity has become ingrained in Canadian society. We are Canadians, not because we are from Canada, but because we came from somewhere else.

Today, I choose 'The Tower of Babel' as my theme because I have personally worked as a publisher for the last 10 years, creating a multilingual and multicultural literary anthology called Variety Crossing. My task has been to encourage writers to submit works in their mother language, and then translate those works into English or Korean. I do this because I believe that literature and friendship go hand in hand. When a writer expresses something that they feel is important, they are sharing it with others in the enthusiastic belief that it is something others should hear. Differences in language, however, always seem to get in the way.

The problem can be traced back to the Tower of Babel. The Book of Genesis reminds us that we all once spoke the same language. Ideas were limited because there was only so much one could say with a limited vocabulary. Repetition ruled in place of innovation.

Mankind attempted to build a Tower, working together without conflict to share a common goal – to reach Heaven without the help of God. This was not in God's plans, however, and so He created a way to disperse the people and obey Him again. He created languages.

Something else happened on that fateful day. What God assumed to be Babel actually became the roots of what we now call multiculturalism. And it was good. For it helped us all understand that it is not sameness which helps us grow, but embracing differences that make us all better people.

There are critics of multiculturalism in Canada who argue that any government-sponsored program cannot be good for the nature under which culture develops. They believe that artists should be allowed to find their own voices without being told what to write, how to write it, or how to share the written arts with others. Culture, growing on its own, to them, is sacrosanct.

The problem with this argument is that it measures political and financial encouragement in terms of results that are simply misread. In fact, most writers would be offended if anyone told them what to say, or for that matter where or how they should say it. Fortunately, we live in a society where we can ignore narrow-minded propaganda and make our own decisions.

We are a gathering of poets, essayist, novelist and writers, brought together in the anthology by an energetic KCLF-21 Press, to share in the passion of hearing what we each have to say. And we don't consider differences of language a handicap. We consider it a blessing. We have finally bridged the gap created in Babel. Today, we can hear not only the voices of others, but also the rhythms, words and ideas. We can respect them. And we can also understand them.

Embracing the cultures of our neighbours has taught us how to better see the world. We learn from our differences. And we grow. What is even more beautiful is that no one has stopped us and told us what to think or what to say. We are simply being ourselves.

One of my passions today is to take the words of poets and translate their ideas into Korean. All cultures have a wonderful music in their own language. Trying to capture that music and turn it into a melody my brothers and sisters can understand is what excites me.

I have lived through many songs. War, poverty, peace, despair and hope. Each song has helped give me some of the notes to translate the feelings that I read from people of other lands. The feelings are not perfect, however. Sometimes it is difficult to capture the delicate echoes of a birdsong on Edward Garden's hillside. Or the footfalls of a ghost stumbling through the war-torn landscape of its homeland.

Babel limits me. But it can never stop me from drawing upon sounds from my own language to help sing the words of others. There's a profound beauty in the experiences of others that deserves my most humble attempts at exposing those moments to others.

If the Story of Babel taught us nothing more, I hope that it at least taught us to take an extra moment and listen to others, regardless of their background.

After all, it is easy to blame everything on how different we are. It is more difficult to understand that we all came from the same place, and it's actually these differences that make us all the same.

Recently, Dalton McGuinty, Premier of Ontario, in his personal message wrote that: Ontario's and Canada's strength comes from the diversity and knowledge of its people. Variety Crossing is a multicultural collection of poetry, essays and writings by Canadian of all backgrounds. My colleagues and I appreciate the significant role the anthology plays in promoting diversity cross the country.

> *"Poetry often allows us to see into the mind of the poet, it is a wonderful way of introducing people of one culture to people of another."*
> *- David Macfarlane, newspaper columnist and past contributor to Variety Crossing*

*"Canada is blessed with many acclaimed writers, working in a wide variety of styles and languages. An anthology like Variety Crossing is a powerful demonstration of how rich and varied Canadian culture truly is. This collection also plays a valuable role as a bridge between artists and their audiences." - Sheila Copps, former Minister of Canadian Heritage*

I publish Variety Crossing for one simple reason: it is a cultural bridge. It joins together all our cultures, languages and races as one, without the obstacles created in Babel. We are all neighbours, living together without walls. It celebrates the diversity that we must all embrace.

And nowhere is this diversity more apparent or important than in my city of Toronto. And that's what makes the city so exciting and vibrant. Everywhere you walk, you discover how well cultures come together. On every street, you see different cultures meet face-to-face: the culture of ideas, the culture of art, the culture of clothing and the culture of food. And each street is a symphony of words, with hundreds of mother tongues filling the air. In our city, these cultures are exchanged by the minute, helping us all embrace, accept and respect the differences we face in our daily lives. The best part is that in a city like Toronto, in a country like Canada, where these differences become part of our daily fabric, we don't notice these differences any more. In fact, we come to expect them. Because that is what being a Canadian really is.

Being a Canadian is also about embracing every moment that you are a guest in a foreign land. We, the KCLF-21 Press, are very proud to have "Stories that bind", The International Festival and Conference. We are also proud to present to you our special 10th anniversary volume of Variety Crossing.

Friends, as the river of stars brightens the night sky, let this world, too, become bright with stars of hope. Let us welcome peace and cherish hope using our pens and our collective wisdom.

# Introduction

## Ten More Years! A Multicultural Collaboration Worth Celebrating AND Continuing

PRISCILA UPPAL

My co-vivant Christopher Doda and I decided twelve years ago that once we had hit the milestone of our ten-year anniversary, we would celebrate with a big party. This decision was motivated by two factors: one, neither of us had any interest in joining the formal institution of marriage; and, two, we had been to countless weddings of family and friends that had since fallen to pieces—as had so many marriages before our time entered into by older relatives and friends—that we felt people should not make such a fuss over beginning relationships, but should reserve their champagne and chocolates and fondue pots for those couples who had accomplished a sustained love over time.

The same rationale might equally be employed in terms of celebrating literary journals. New journals and magazines frequently start up with great fanfare, enthusiasm, and funding, often by individuals or collectives anxious to have their voices published and respected, as well as by those seeking to invigorate the current cultural climate with new, challenging, or provocative art. But it is very difficult to sustain a literary journal beyond a few years—financially, artistically, editorially—and many fold within a half-decade, leaving well-intentioned editors and writers disillusioned, unhappy, and destined for obscurity again. It might very well be harder to keep a literary journal alive than a modern marriage.

But Dae-Tong Huh and the Korean-Canadian Literary Forum-21 Press have done just that. With this publication, Variety Crossing turns ten years-old. Ten years. Ten volumes. And so, when Dae-Tong Huh invited me to write the introduction to this landmark issue, I thought yes, ten years is worth celebrating, but I also brought my let's see what you've accomplished in those ten years attitude with me.

Of course, I already knew that Variety Crossing had accomplished a great deal. I have been involved with the magazine, as a contributing poet, a subscriber, and supporter, for the last five years. But since I was not involved with the publication since its inception (I only became aware of it when I was invited to submit poetry to it in 2003), I requested that I be supplied with all previous issues to get a better picture of how the journal had started and how its vision as well as production had changed over the years.

Here are some of my findings:

Published in 1999 by the Baek-Ji Literary Club, Volume One of the journal was 128 pages, and almost all the featured poetry and prose were in Korean by members of the club, such as S.B. Chung, H.S. Byun, H.G. Oh, and B.H. Choi; only a few poems in English by Paul Saltzman, President of Sunrise Films Ltd., appeared. Photos of the authors lined the back cover. Sang-Bin Nahm was President of the club, and Dae-Tong Huh, looking rather distinguished and proud, was one of the club's members.

By the publication of Volume Two, already much had changed to broaden the community associated with the magazine as well as its scope and mandate. In his preface, Dae-Tong Huh, now President of the newly-renamed Korean-Canadian Literary Club, writes: "Our club has grown from a handful of writers dedicated to writing poetry, essays, and short stories to a garden of writers from many different cultures and age groups." Almost all the included pieces in Korean and English also appeared in translation (Korean to English and vice versa). The English-Canadian journalist David MacFarlane embraced the journal as a way for diverse groups in Canada to learn more about each other. Although Canada is noted for its multiculturalism and diversity, he admits "we do not know quite enough about one another," and argues that poetry can help us bridge these gaps, as it "introduces us to worlds that we do not otherwise have access to." And I must agree with MacFarlane about this, as I have to confess that before Variety Crossing I had never read poems by Canadians that were originally written in Korean. And yet there are many Korean-Canadian poets working in Canada, and many who are also involved in translating English and other-language works into Korean (a time-consuming and usually thankless task). I was deeply moved by the poetry of writer and translator Helen Kang, whose speaker in a poem called "Shout" hears a voice telling her, "to get married rather than go to graduate school,/that reassured me that silence is a woman's way to happiness." It is a voice echoing still in the heads of dozens of my female students at York University, many of whom are the first in their families to attend post-secondary education, often without their parents' approval. It is also worth noting that literary translation remains an undervalued and under-funded practice in Canada. Mainstream publishing houses print very few, if any, books in translation, even between our two official languages. Therefore, to facilitate and represent translation in Variety Crossing, continues to be one of its most important and distinguishing editorial mandates.

With Volume Three, the production values clearly improved: the paper, the fonts, the layout, and the cover, which included French flaps, were more professionally handled. Dae-Tong Huh's introduction waxed poetically over the important "gift" of multiculturalism—I should mention here that I don't think I have ever heard anyone speak with so much love and faith about multiculturalism than Mr. Huh—and this ideal is reflected in the magazine through its gradual increase in the number of translated languages featured in each issue. With this issue the bilingual journal became trilingual with the inclusion of French.

By Volume Four the journal was clearly multi-lingual. Book-length now (over two-hundred pages), the cover was no longer a basic functional necessity but another space for expression—fish and leaves swirling through the air, tiny people jumping and running across the page, words flowing out of one of these book-athletes. This issue also included various

Canadian and international heavyweight authors, such as English-Canadian writer Barry Callaghan and Russian poet Yevgeny Yevtushenko. The tone was more confident, assured and, at times, brassy. The non-fiction essays even courted controversy (see Elizabeth Coelho's politically-motivated piece, "Raising Bilingual Children").

By Volume Five, the range of voices had expanded again. Between this issue's covers, I count forty-one writers from all different cultural and linguistic backgrounds. Noted French-Canadian writer Nicole Brossard appeared in French, English, and Korean. Serbian was included. This was the first issue, as it is now, divided into genres, and featured a "Youth Corner"—a great initiative to foster young talent. David MacFarlane, in his introduction, cheers: "this is exactly the kind of cultural project that makes living in a city such as Toronto so exciting." Volume Five is also the first issue in which I appeared as an "invited poet." I was honoured to have been asked to contribute and was immediately welcomed by Dae-Tong Huh, the translators, and the entire Variety Crossing community. What a thrill and at the same time a humbling experience to see my work in a language I cannot read. And Korean characters seem to me to be so fragile, elegant, and lyrical; a perfect vehicle for the precarious nature of poetry.

Authors names began to appear on the cover in Volume Six, an indication that the publisher and editors believe these names had now entered the public consciousness, and that they had succeeded in identifying a growing reading community for their works. A political consciousness permeated the issue, which opened with a substantial interview with filmmaker Brian McKenna about his documentary Korea, The Unfinished War, and includes a poem by George Elliot Clarke about former Canadian Prime Minister Pierre Elliott Trudeau.

By Volume Seven the magazine donned a modernist geometric piece on its cover. Author photos were abandoned, another vote of confidence that the work stands on its own merit. To highlight this volume and the important cultural contribution Variety Crossing had made thus far, Prof.

Richard Teleky and I organized a launch at York University as part of our annual Ethnicity and Literature mini-conference series. Dae-Tong Huh and translator Mina Cho gave short lectures, and a spirited and provocative panel discussion ensured as we explored to a group challenges of writing literature in a new country and the factors that contribute to a group's ability to be heard. Our students, who had little exposure to Korean-Canadian culture, let alone to its poetry and prose, benefited greatly from the experience, many acquiring a new respect for and interest in the process of translation.

Ontario Premier Dalton McGuinty contributed an essay on multiculturalism for Volume Eight: "The more I learn about people, the more I understand that deep down, we are all the same, with the same basic hopes and fears. We want the same things—to live in peace and build a better future." The rest of the issue bore out the Premier's claims, and at the launch at the University of Toronto, contributing authors—including myself and good friend poet Sonnet L'Abbé—went up to the stage to act out sections from George Elliott Clarke's new play about Trudeau. Piano music, dance, and more literary readings rounded out the evening. Plus, as always, a jubilant recitation of a Korean folk song, with phonetic lyrics provided for all to join in. And then photographs.

The range of languages and voices that appeared in Volume Nine is truly outstanding. In addition to Korean, English and French, there was also Romanian, Polish, and Ojibwe. It is, unfortunately, still rare to find Native poetry and prose alongside other Canadian authors' works, and so the contributions of Linda McGregor and Marion McGregor were a significant inclusion. In "On Dreamer's Rock: A Place of Visions and Dreams," we readers are witnesses as: "The youth await their Spirit Guides to appear and announce/Whether they be a scout, messenger, warrior/ Hunter, skilled trapper, fisherman, great leader,/Medicine man, seer or spiritual counselor." Reading through this issue, one has the feeling that our destinies are contained within its covers, and that these paths are richly lined with varied, unique possibilities. As Mr. Huh insists, "All we have to do is keep our hearts, eyes, and ears open and ready for the music, for the Ethnic Dialogue."

As for what gifts and surprises Volume Ten contains, dear reader, I will discover these with you. I love the fact that I won't know what language I will encounter or what beautiful accents and scripts will pepper the pages, or what insights on life and its various tragicomic elements might be offered until I open the covers. While each issue has grown further and dug deeper roots than the one before it, there is no predicting the content of future volumes. Like culture, Variety Crossing learns and exchanges with each of its authors, translators, editors, and readers, transforming itself into a new, vibrant incarnation of life.

When my co-vivant and I reached our ten-year benchmark in the summer of 06, we threw a huge party in our home and invited family, friends, and close colleagues and students to celebrate with lots of wine, good food, and cheer. When the time arrived for speeches, I recited a poem that I had written for the occasion, and then I presented Chris with T-shirts I'd had made for both of us. They said: Ten More Years! on one side and Happily Unmarried Since 1996 on the other. The owner of the store liked them so much she hung them in the window until I came to pick them up. I suppose I could order T-shirts trumpeting Variety Crossing's many accomplishments over the past decade but I think we might do better to celebrate the journal in more substantial and lasting ways. Running a literary journal is Sisyphean at the best of times; when you add to that the necessity of acquiring literary translators of many languages to execute this unique, multilingual and multicultural format and mandate, the challenges double and triple in number. Support this publication however you can—as a fundraiser, a reader, a writer, a subscriber, a librarian, a politician, a translator, a teacher. Tell others about it. Buy a few and pass them out in your neighbourhood. With the publication of the Ten-year Anniversary Issue, Variety Crossing isn't soliciting our interest and gratitude; it has already earned it.

# 서언

## 십년을 더 내다보며!
## 복합문화가 함께하는 뜻있는 경축과 지속성

프리실라 우빨

12년 전, 나의삶에 파트너 크리스토퍼 도다와 나는 우리의 10 주년 기념일을 큰 파티로 기념하기로 결정했다. 이 동기는 두 가지 이유에서였다: 첫번째는 우리는 결혼이라는 형식적인 제도에 얽매이는데 관심이 없었고, 두번째 이유는, 우리가 참석했던 많은 친척과 친구들의 결혼식이 실패로 끝난 것을 보아 왔는데—우리세대의 옛 친척과 친구들의 많은 결혼에서 보았듯이—우리는 시작부터 떠들썩할 필요가 없다는 이유에서였다. 그러나 커플을 위한 샴페인, 초콜릿과 폰듀그릇 등은 사랑의 표시로 오랫동안 보유해야 한다고 생각한다.

문학저널을 기념하는데에 있어서도 같은 비유를 적용하고자 한다. 대다수의 문예저널은 화려한 취지, 열성과 자금을 가지고 시작하는데, 이들 개인이나 집단에서 발견되는 공통점은 그들의 목소리가 출판되어 대중들로부터 존중 받으려는 기대에 초점을 맞추고 있다. 뿐만 아니라 이들이 보는 새롭고, 도전적이며, 또한 자극적인 현세의 문화풍조에 활기를 뛰게 하는데도 관심을 쏟고 있다. 그렇지만 이러한 문예지가 몇년을

지탱하지 못하는 이유는— 경제적, 예술적면에서나, 편집하는 과정에서 많은 어려움을 만나게 되기 때문이다. 그래서 대 다수의 저널은 이와같은 어려움들을 넘기지 못하고 5년내에 문을 닫는다. 결과는 선의의 편집인들, 문인들이 환멸과 불행으로 떠나게 하는 결과를 초래한다. 이런점에서 문예지는 현시대의 결혼보다 계속하기란 참으로 어렵다.

하지만 허대통씨와 한카문학비영리출판사는 이를 잘 해 내고

있다. 버라이어티 크로싱 복합문예지 출판은 금년이 10년째다. 10년에 10집을 출간했다.
그래서 허대통 발행인은 랜드마크로 나에게 서언을 써 주기를 의뢰 해 왔을때, 내가 10년을 기념할 만한 가치가 있는지, 승락을 생각하면서 나 역시 그가 일구어낸 지난 10년 동안의 업적이 무엇이였나를 생각케 했다.

내가 이미 알고 있는 바로는 버라이어티 크로싱 복합문예지는 많은 성취를 했다. 나는 이 저널에, 지난 5년동안 한 시인의 참여자로, 구독자, 후원자로 연계를 가져 왔다. 그러나 이 잡지 발간 처음부터 참여하지 않았기 때문에(나의 시 참여는 지난 2003년 부터였기에), 나는 그 전의 잡지의 내용을 드려다 보기 위하여 필요한 버라이어티 크로싱 문예지 전부(2003년전)를 보내 달라고 요청했다. 이 잡지는 어떻게 시작 했으며 어떠한 비전과 목표를 가지고 지난 수 년간의 출판 변화를 가져 왔는지 알기 위해서였다.

나는 이 문예지에서 몇가지를 발견했다 - 1999년 백지문학회가 출판한 제 1집은 128페이지였다. 이 문예지가 담고 있는 시와 수필은 거의 모두가 한국문인 멤버들의 글을 담고 있었다, S.B. Chang, H. S.Byun,H.G. Oh와 최봉호 시인, 썬라이스 영화사 사장 폴 쌀즈만의 몇개의 영시가 포함 되었으며, 작가들의 사진을 책 뒷표지에 담고 있었다. 그 당시 회장은 남상빈씨였다. 품위와 긍지를 가진 허대통씨는 문학회 멤버였다.

출판한 제2집 잡지에는 이미 공동체을 향하여 범위을 넓였으며 잡지의 출판을 이 초점에 맞추어 임무수행에 많은 변화가 있었음을 눈여겨 볼수 있었다. 한카문학회의 새로운 회장인 허대통회장은 책의 말머리에서, "본 문학회는 많은 다른 문화와 연령을 망라하여 작가들의 정원에서 자라온 자랑스런 풍성한 시, 수필과 단편들로 부터 자라왔습니다." 라고 쓰여있다. 거의 작품들은 영어와 한글, 두언어로 번역되었다 (영어에서 한글, 또는 반대로). 영국계 캐네디언, 저널리스트 데이비드 멕팔레인은 "캐나다의 다양한 시민들을 위한 길로 이 저널은 서로를 이해 하는데 도움을 준다."라고 시사하고 있다. 비록 캐나다가 복합문화와 다양성에 대하여 관심을 가지고 있지만, "

우리는 서로를 잘 모른다" 그런데 시는 그 공백을 메꾸어준다. 이와 같이 "세계로 우리를 소개하는 길은 이 방법외에는 다른 돌출구가 없다." 했는데 나도 그와 같은 생각이다. 나의 솔직한 고백은 원어인 한국어로 쓰여진 글을 읽어 본 적이 없었다. 물론 한국계 캐네디언 시인들이 많이 캐나다에 활동하고 있음을 알고있다.(시간관계상 대부분 관심이 없는). 시도 쓰며 번역가인 강헬렌의 "외침(shout)" 란 시가 그녀에게 들려오는, "대학원 진학 보다는 결혼하면 어떨까, / 침묵은 여성들의 행복으로 가는 길." 이 시에서
나는 깊은 감명을 받았다. 아직도 요크대학의 수 많은 여학생들 머릿속에 이 음성이 아직도 메아리치고 있다.
가족중 처음으로 대학에 들어간 대부분의 학생들은 부모들의 지원없이 대학공부를 한다.
여기서 짚고 넘어야할 점은 번역문학은 캐나다에서 아직까지 과소평가 받고있으며 재정 지원을 하지 않는다. 주류 출판사는 캐나다의 공용어로 번역하여 출판하는 책은 아주 소수에 불과하다. 그래서, 버라이어티 크로싱 복합문예지에 초점을 맞춘 번역은 편집자의 중요하고도 특징적인 임무 중의 하나로 계속 되어야 겠다.
제3집 제작은 확실히 변모 되었다: 종이, 글자체, 레이아웃, 커버와 부채질하는 듯 하는 불어, 이 모두 다 전문적으로 처리되었다. 허대통 회장의 머리말은 복합문화의 "선물 의—중요성을 시적으로 표현했다. 여기서 나는 허회장만큼이나 복합문화에 그 많은 사랑과 믿음으로 말하는 사람을 만나 본적이 없었다 - 이 이상은 문예집마다에 포함된 여러 언어의 수가 점차 늘어남에서 나타난다. 이 3집은 2개국에서 불어를 포함시키면서 3개국어로 출판되었다.

제4집은 확실히 복합언어로 출판되었다. 책의 길이로 보면(200 페이지가 넘는).
책의 커버는 기본적이고 실용적인 필요성 뿐만 아니라 또 다른 표현의 공간이었다 — 공중을 소용돌이치는 물고기와 나뭇잎들, 페이지를 건너 뛰는 작은 사람들, 이 책표지에
운동선수로부터 흘러나오는 단어들.
제 4집은 영어권의 여러 캐나다 작가들과 세계적인 작가들로, 영국계-

캐네디언 작가 배리 칼라한과 러시안 시인 예브겐니 예프트첸코들이 포함 되었다. 문예지의 어조는 더 자신감이 넘쳐나고, 확실하고 때로는 자신만만함까지 덧보여준다. 논픽션 수필 작품 중에는 코트의 논쟁까지 실리고 있다 (엘리자베스 꼬엘호의 정치적 동기가 부여된 " 이중언어의 자녀교육"을 참고).

제5집의 목소리의 범위는 더 광범해졌다. 이 책표지에는 문화적이며, 언어가 다른 배경의 41명의 작가들을 한눈으로 보게된다. 불어권-캐네디언 저명한 작가 니콜 브로싸르 글은 불어, 영어, 한글로 출판됐다. 서비안어도 포함 되어 있다. 제5집이 문학장르로 나누어진 것은 처음인데 "틴의 코너"("youth corner")는 틴의 재능을 키우는데 필요한 대단한 독창력이다. 데이빗 맥파렌인은 그의 서언에서 " 버라이어티 크로싱의 출판은 토론토와 같은 도시에 살고 있는 모든 종족들간의 삶을 살찌게 하는 문화의 설계이기에 더욱 흥미롭게 합니다" 격려의 갈채를 보낸다고 했다. 그리고 나는 처음으로 제5집에 "초대시인"으로 초대되었다. 나는 기고해 달라는 허대통 번역가와 버라이어티 공동체의 영예로운 환영을 얻게 된 것이다. 내가 읽을수 없는 언어로 번역된 나의 글을 보는것은 스릴과 겸허한 느낌까지 경험케했다. 한글 문자는 나에겐 섬세하고, 우아하고, 감상적으로 보인다; 시의 불확실한 특성을 위한 완벽한 수레인것 처럼 보인다.

제 6집 앞표지에 작가들의 이름이 나타난다. 발행자와 편집자는 이들 작가들의 이름이 이제 대중 의식을 감안하고 또한 이 잡지를 읽는 독자 공동체를 넓여가는데 성공했다. 영화 제작자 브라이언 맥케나의 – 그의 한국 전쟁에 관한 다큐멘터리, "끝나지 않은 전쟁"에 관한 인터뷰로 시작하여 조지 엘리엇트 클락이 쓴 캐나다 전수상 피에르 엘리어트 트루도에 관한 드라마와 그의 시를 포함시켰다.

제7집의 커버표지는 현대풍의 기하학적 도형들로 채워졌다. 작가 사진들은 없어지고 글들은 문학적 가치로 홀로서기 할 수 있다는 믿음을 표시한다. 버라이어티 크로싱 제 7집과 그때까지 쌓아온 중요한 문화적 공헌을 돋보이게 하기 위해 리챠드 텔레키 교수와 나는 요크대학에서 해마다 하는 소수민족과

문학 미니 컨퍼런스 시리즈의 한 부분으로 버라이어티 크로싱 출판기념회를 가졌다. 허대통 발행인과 조미나 번역가는 짧은 강의를 했는데 활기에 넘치고 자극적인 공개토론을 하는 동안 확인된 바는, 새로운 나라에 와서 문학 작품을 쓰는 도전과 그 요인을 탐구 하자는데 있었으며 이것은

그룹토론의 능력을 기르자는데 그 요점이 있었다. 한국계 캐네디언 문화를 접촉케된 요크대 학생들에게는 시와 수필에 대한 좋은 경험이었고 번역과정의 관심도와 그에대한 새로운 중요성을 취득케 했다.

온타리오 주 수상 달턴 맥퀸티는 제8집에서 다문화성에 관한 수필을 기고했다: "내가 사람들에 관해 더 많은 것을 배우고, 깊이 이해하면 할수록, 우리는 희망과 공포를 가지고 살아가는, 동일한 인간조건 임을 이해하게 되며 우리는 다 같이 우리 자손들이 평화롭고 보다 좋은 삶을 영위하도록 기대합니다." 잡지는 맥긴티의 주장을 뒷받침해 주었고, 토론토 대학에서 출판기념회가 있었는데 나와 친구 소넷 라베와 같은 작가들은 무대에 올라가 조지 엘리엇 클락이 쓴 투루도에 관한 새로운 연극을 연기했다. 피아노 연주, 춤, 그리고 시와 수필 낭송으로 밤은 깊어갔다. 그리고 항상 그랬듯이, 모두가 참여할 수 있도록 프로그램의 가사가 프린트된 한국 민요 아리랑을 힘차게 불렀고 사진을 촬영했다.

제9집에 실린 언어와 표현 범위는 괄목 할만치, 한글, 영어, 불어와 로마니어, 폴랜드어, 오집어(원주민어)도 담았다. 안타깝게도 캐나다 원주민의 시가 다른 캐네디언 작가들의 작품과 같이 출판되는 것은 아직까지는 거의 찾기 어려웠다. 그래서 린다 맥그래거와 마리언 맥그래거의 작품들이 더더욱 뜻깊은 기고임에 틀림없다. "꿈꾸는이의 바위: 시각과 꿈의 장소." 독자의 증인으로서: " 그들의 영적 안내자로 젊음을 사르고 기다리는 내용을 담고있는데, "정찰, 메신저, 무인 또는 사냥꾼, 덫을 놓는 노련한 사람, 어부, 훌륭한 지도자, /의사, 예언자 또는 영적인 카운슬러."들이다. 시를 읽으면서 한가지

와닿는 것은 우리들의 지향이 커버페이지에 담겨져 있다는 것이다. 이 길들은 여러모로 다르고, 독득한 가능성들로 채우고있다. 허대통씨가 주장 하듯이 "우리 모두는 소수민족들의 대화를 위하여, 우리의 가슴,

눈, 귀를 열어 이 음악을 들을 준비가 필요하다."

제10집이 안겨줄 선물과 놀람에 대해서는 나와 독자 여러분은 곧 알게 될 것이다. 어떤 언어가 더 첨가될지, 어떤 아름다운 엑센트의 글과 각본이 페이지를 장식할 것인지, 또는 인생과 희비극적인 요소들에 관한 어떠한 통찰이 나에게 주어질지 표지를 열때까지 예상할 수 없다. 각 문예지마다 계속 성장해 왔으며 그에 앞서 이 문예지는 더 깊은 뿌리를 파고 들어간다. 문화와 같이, 버리이어티 크로싱문예지는 작가들, 번역가들, 편집자들, 독자들 모두가 배우고 나누면서, 새롭고 더욱 빛나는 삶으로 우리를 변화 시킨다.

나의 삶의 파트너와 나는 2006년 여름, 십년이 되었을때 가족과 친구, 가까운 동료와 학생들을 집으로 초대하여 와인과 맛있는 요리와 환호의 기분으로 큰 파티를 열었다. 인사말을 할 시간이 왔을때, 그날을 위해 쓴 특별한 시를 낭송했다. 그리고 크리스에게 우리를 위해 내가 특별히 만든 티셔츠를 선물했다. 말한데로: 티셔츠 한면엔 "십년더!"라고 써 있었고, 다른면엔 "1996년부터 행복한 미혼" 이라고 써 넣었다. 주문한 가게 주인은 티셔츠가 너무 마음에 들었든지 내가 찾으러 갈때까지 가게 창문에 티셔츠를 걸어 놓았다. 십년동안의 버라이어티 크로싱의 많은 성과를 축하하기 위해 티셔츠를 주문할 필요는 없겠지만, 그것보다 더 더중요한 것은 실질적이고 영속적 길을 위하여 축하하는것이 낳을것 같다. 문학잡지를 운영하는 것은 제일 왕성한 시기에도 끝없는 헛수고처럼 보인다.

그 위에 이 독특한 복합, 다문화적인 포맷과 임무을 실행하기 위해 번역자들을 찾는 어려움은 두, 세배 힘이 들것이다. 이 출판을 어떤 방법으로써 지원하겠는가 – 기금 주달자로, 독자로서, 작가로서, 구독자로, 도서관원으로, 정치가로, 번역자로, 선생으로. 다른 사람들한테 알려라. 몇권을 구입해서 동네이웃에게 전해줘라. 버라이어티 크로싱의 10주년 기념호를 출판하면서, 버리이어티 크로싱문예지는 우리의 관심과 사의를 구걸하는 것은 아니다; 이미 그 한계를 넘어섰다.

*Translated by Dae-Tong Huh and Hyeamin Yoon.*

# Poetry

# Poème de Nicole Brossard

Nicole Brossard

Je m'intéresse à la connaissance parce que
je voudrais de l'univers soigner le sens
autour d'une femme et de plusieurs. Oui,
c'est rapproché de la parole d'honneur
que le désir peut rendre dicible la comparaison
que nous faisons entre la mer et nos intentions
de bonheur. Je m'intéresse à la connaissance
parce que trop de vie nous échappe
lorsque nous exerçons notre faculté de joie

*Extrait du recueil Langues obscures, Éditions de l'Hexagone, Montréal, 1992.*

# Poem by Nicole Brossard

Nicole Brossard

I indulge in knowledge because I would like to
nurture the sense in the universe surrounding
one and several women. Yes, it's close to the
word of honour that desire can fin words for
the comparison that we draw between the sea
and our intentions for happiness. I indulge in
knowledge because too much of life eludes us
when we exercise our capacity for joy

*Translated by Louise Forsyth. Excerpt from Mobility of light, selected poems edited by Louise Forsyth. To come out in fall 2008.*

# 니콜 브로샤드의 시

니콜 브로샤드

나는 앎에 욕심이 있어요 만물의 오감이
주변의 여성들을 위해 영양분이 되길
바라기 때문이지요. 그래요, 그것은
욕망이 탐익할 수 있는 영예로운 말은
행복을 위한 바다와 우리의 의지 사이에서
파생되는 비교를 위한 낱말에 가깝습니다.
나는 앎에 욕심이 있습니다 즐거움만의 추구
이런 삶은 우리를 외면 하기 때문이지요

*Korean translation by Dae-Tong Huh.*

시 선집, 빛의 가동성에서 발췌, 루이스 포시즈 편집. 2008년 가을에 출판

# Poème de Nicole Brossard

NICOLE BROSSARD

ce sont toujours les mêmes mots
grands objets de paroles
lumière nuit ou silence
les mêmes oiseaux l'après-midi
le bruit de l'automne un autre
paragraphe en deçà des mots
quand je respire
la réponse qui fuit

*Extrait du recueil Au présent des veines, Éditions Écrits des Forges, Trois-Rivières, 2003.*

## Poem by Nicole Brossard

Nicole Brossard

they are always the same words
large spoken objects
light night or silence
the same birds the afternoon
the sound of autumn another
paragraph on the intimate side of words
when I breathe
the fleeting response

*English translation by Louise Forsyth.*
*Excerpt from Mobility of light, selected poems edited by Louise Forsyth. To come out in fall 2008.*

# 니콜 브로샤드의 시

## 니콜 브로샤드

항상 동일한 낱말
빈번한 담화의 대상들
은은한 밤 또는 침묵
오후에 나르는 같은 새들
가을의 울음소리 또 다른
낱말이 암시하는 절(節)
내가 호흡할때 떠어오르는
순간의 응답이다

*Korean translation by Dae-Tong Huh.*
시 선집, 빛의 가동성에서 발췌, 루이스 포시즈 편집. 2008년 가을에 출판

# "Camille 2000"

## à la manière de Piero Piccioni (to de Piero Piccioni)

George Elliott Clarke

As material and as immaterial as ink,
As dazzling and as weighty as snow—

Our words—
Our tears—

Ulcerous tints,
Moist brilliance,

Sweet spite in our commingling —
Our kindred glances, communicating.

I scuttle to-and-fro: an ambassador;
You shuttle back-and-forth, negotiating.

Shoulder blades rise and plunge like two knives—
Eyes correspond.

Words well up in liquid clusters,
Spilling glitter in a white arena—this sheet.

*"Camille 2000" is a 1970 film by Radley Metzger, a U.S. director based in Italy at the time: it's a story about 1960s sexual relationships.*

# "카밀 2000"

## 피에로 피시온니에게

**죠지 엘리엇트 클락**

잉크처럼 본질이며 본질이 아닌,
눈처럼 부시며 무거운—

우리의 언어들—
우리의 눈물들—

궤양의 담채,
눅눅한 광택

우리의 달콤한 혼합에 짓궂임—
우리의 친근한 눈짓, 대화다.

나는 허둥대는: 대사:
너는 협상의 앞뒤 창구다.

견갑골 날개가 두개의 칼처럼 상승과 하락—
눈은 응시한다.

낱말은 액체송이로 솟아나,
백색 경기장에 반짝이는 유출— 이 지면.

*Translated by Dae-Tong Huh.*

카멜 2000: 1970년대 영화 미국 영화제작가 래들리 메즈거의 작품 그시대 이태리를 배경으로 한 1960 년대의 성에 관한 스토리.

# "Malinconica Serenità"
## à la manière d'Ennio Morricone

George Elliott Clarke

Unblemished wine!
Wine with a tiger's growling spirit!
Some contumacious nectar....

An elegant, dusky maid, smelling of lilies—
A black-silk Creole splurging on perfume—
I mean, smoky with perfume—

A majesty to relish like licorice—
To ravish and shiver honey within—
A slippery, alert, unimpaired, and dexterous maw.

Floods of gold-plated wine!
Showers of lily-scented perfume!
Kisses pooling, then swamping lips!

Untarnished blackness, pure girlish lust,
Then oiled ebony poling a citrus cleft.

*Piccioni and Morricone are well-known Italian film music composers of the 1960s and 1970s.*

# "우울증의 고요함"

## 엔니오 모리코니에게

### 조지 엘리엇트 클락

단백한 포도주여!
호랑이 원기를 내는 포도주여!
상당이 오만한 과즙이로다…

우아하고, 거무스레한 하녀, 백합냄새가 풍기는—
까만 실크에 향수가 밴 크리올 사람의 과시—
나는 향수의 연기를 말함이다—

감초처럼 짙은 향기의 풍김—
매혹하는 전율 꿀 맛—
미끄럽고, 민첩하며, 줄지않는, 기민한 동물의 입

도금병에 담긴 포도주의 홍수여라!
백합 향수의 샤워여!
키스의 봇물, 늪의 입술 이어라!

음융하고 순결한 소녀다운 정욕,
터진 감귤을 자극하는 흑단.

*Translated by Dae-Tong Huh*
*Piccioni and Morricone*는 1960 - 1970년대의 이탈리아의 저명한 영화작곡가들

## A Poet's Heart

Ko Un

A poet is born in a chink of crimes,
Larceny, murder, fraud, or violence,
In some obscure corner of the world.

First the poet's words go creeping
Into chinks in harsh cursing's foulest oaths
Heard in a city's poorest roughest slums,
And for a time dominate society.
Then the poet's heart fashions a single cry
Out of all today's truths as they come seeping
Through chinks in the evil and lies,
And gets beaten to death by other hearts.

A poet's heart is doomed, that's sure.

# Sunlight

Ko Un

It's absolutely inevitable!
So just take a deep breath
and accept this adversity.
But look!
A distinguished visitor deigns to visit
my tiny north-facing cell.
Not the chief making his rounds, no,
but a ray of sunlight as evening falls,
a gleam no bigger than a screwed-up stamp.
A sweetheart fit to go crazy about.
It settles there on the palm of a hand,
warms the toes of a shyly bared foot.
Then as I kneel and, undevoutly,
offer it a dry, parched face to kiss,
in a moment that scrap of sunlight slips away.
After the guest has departed through the bars,
the room feels several times colder and darker.
This military prison special cell
is a photographer's darkroom.
Without any sunlight I laughed like a fool.
One day it was a coffin holding a corpse.
One day it was altogether the sea.
A wonderful thing!
A few people survive here.

Being alive is a sea
without a single sail in sight.

# 일인층 슬프다

고은

슬프다 깨달음은 어느새 모순이 된다
지난 세기 초
혁명 뒤 소비에트 시인들은
' 우리들'이라고만 말하기로 했다
'우리들'이라고만
시인 자신을 부르기로 했다
황홀했다
그 결정은
폭설 때문에
거리에 나가지 못한 채
방안에 서성거릴 때도 유효했다
저 혼자
'우리들…,' 이라고 맹세했다
거울 저쪽에서
'나'는 어디론가 사라졌다
어느 화창한 날 뛰쳐나온 마야코프스키도
'우리들'이라고 외치고 외쳤다
그는 거리의 시인이었다
어디에도 '나'는 허용되지 않았다
'나'는 죄악이었다
'우리들'
'우리들…,'
오직 그것만이 주문(呪文)의 권력이 되었다.

차츰 하늘의 저기압이 눌러댔다
여름 꽃들 누누이 짓밟혔다
혁명은 혁명을 먹었다

모든 아이들의 공에서 바람이 빠져갔다
'우리들'도
팽팽한 대기 속에서 바람이 빠져갔다
누가 대담하게

'나는 사랑한다고 썼으나
아직
'우리들은 사랑한다'라고 읽는 습관이 남아 있었다
겨울 눈이 다 녹지 않았다.
봄은 늘 불안하다

지난 세기 말
소비에트가 죽었다
바르사바 조약 국가들이
하나하나 떨어져 나갔다

그 이래
시인들에게 온통 '나' 뿐이다
'나'로 시작해서
'나'로 하루가 저물었다
'나' 이외에는
아무것도 없다
신(神)도 '나'의 다른 이름이었다

오늘 환대평양
"우리"와 "나"의 유령들을 무한히 파도에 묻는다.
누가 태어날 것인가
'우리'도 아닌
'나'도 아닌 누가 태어날 것인가
파도는 파도의 무덤이고 파도의 자궁이다

## First Person Sorrowful

Ko Un

I am sad. Enlightenment has become so inconsistent.
Early last century
after the Revolution, Soviet poets
decided to only say "We".
Poets decided to only call themselves
"We".
They were ecstatic.
Because of blizzards
That decision
was unable to take to the streets
but it remained valid, lingering doors.
It took oaths, saying "We ..."
all alone.
"I" had disappeared somewhere
beyond the looking glass.
One bright sunny day, Mayakovsky too dashed out
Shouting and shouting "We"
He was a poet of the street.
"I" was not allowed of the street.
"I" was wicked.
"We"
"We ..."
that alone had magic power.

The atmospheric pressure slowly fell lower.
Summer flowers kept being trampled down.
Revolution devoured revolution.

The wind went out of every child's foodball.
Likewise the wind out of the taut atmosphere
of "We ...".
Someone boldly
Wrote "I am in love" but
still
there remained the custom of reading "We are love."
Winter snows had not all melted.
Spring is always uncertain.

Late last century
the Soviet Union died.
The Warsaw Pact countries
quit one after another.

Sine then
poets have nothing at all but "I".
Starting with "I".
There is nothing
except "I".
Even God is only another name for "I".

Today all the Pacific Rim
is endlessly burying in the waves the ghosts of "We" and "I".
What new birth is coming?
What new birth? Neither "We"
nor "I".
Each wave is one wave's tomb, another wave's womb.

# 오늘의 썰물

고은

우리는 기억 하리라
이 세상을 폭풍우로 두들겨 패야 할때가 있다
이 세상을 성난 해일로 덮쳐야 할 때가 있다
비록 흰 거품을 물고 물러서지만
오늘의 썰물로 오늘을 버리지 말자
오늘이야말로 과거와 미래의 실재 아니냐
우리는 기억 하리라
오 끝없는 파도의 민족이여
그러나 이 세상을 한밤중 우는 아이로 달랠 때가 있다
역사가 아버지가 아니라 내 자식일 때가 있다
오늘을 내 자식으로
멀어져가는 썰물의 파도소리로 잠재우건만
그 뿐 아니라 이 세상을 온몸으로 참회할 때가 있다
참회란 땅을 치고 후회하는 게 아니라
하지못한 일을 끝내 해내는 데 있지 않느냐
지금 우리에게 할 일이 있다
우리는 파도치면서 젊은 밀물로 돌아오리라
우리들의 생존 몇 천 년이 오늘이 되어
바다 전체로 온누리로
우리들의 밤을 하나하나 드높은 별빛으로 기억하리라

# Today's Ebb Tide

Ko Un

We shall recall.
There is a time for the world
to be battered by storms,
a time for the world to be covered
with raging waves.
Now white froth goes slowly drifting past
but let's not dismiss today
with the day's ebbing tide.
Today is the stark reality
of past and future.
We shall recall,
We shall recall, and tell our children.
Ah, nation of unending waves!
But there is a time when this world should be lulled,
like a child that cries at midnight.
There is a time when history is not fathers but sons.
I lull today, as if it were my child,
or the ebbing tide's distant repeating waves;
but that's not all, for a time will come
to repent whole-heartedly for what this world is.
Repenting is not a matter of beating the ground
and regretting all the mistakes of the past,
but rather, perhaps, a matter of achieving,
at last, what could not be done before?
Now we have a task to perform.
We'll all return like surging waves

borne on the youthful incoming tide.
Several thousand years of our life
have here become today,
become the whole ocean, become the whole world.
And as we all recall past nights,
each one is somehow a star up there
shining far away.

# I Love You More than Nature

YEVGENY YEVTUSHENKO

I love you more than nature,
Because you are nature itself.
I love you more than freedom,
Because without you freedom is prison.

I love you incautiously,
Like an abyss – not a groove.
I love you more than possible,
And more then impossible too.

I love you timelessly, timelessly
Even being drunk, being rude.
I love you more than myself
I love you more than only you.

I love you more than Shakespeare,
More than all bookish wisdom
Even more than all music,
Because you are music and book.

I love you more than glory of fame, -
Even glory of future times.
I love you more than my Motherland
Because my Motherland is you.

Are you unhappy? About what do you complain?
Don't bother God with your prayers and petitions.
I love you more than happiness. I love you than love

*Translated by Gay Hoaglund with the author (1995).*

## 자연보다 당신을 더 사랑해요

**예브게니 예프뚜센코**

자연보다 당신을 더 사랑합니다,
당신은 자연 자체이기 때문이지요.
자유보다 당신을 더 사랑해요,
당신이 없는 자유는 감옥이기 때문입니다.

사랑해요 당신을 차분한 마음으로,
심연에서 – 습관을 떠나서.
가능한것 보다 더 당신을 사랑할래요,
또한 불가능 보다도 더.

사랑할래요, 영원히 영원히
술취하여, 무례한 행동을 할지라도.
저 자신보다 당신을 더 사랑합니다,
사랑합니다 오직 당신만을.

쎅스피어보다 당신을 더 좋아합니다,
모든 문학의 지혜보다
모든 음악 보다도,
당신은 음악이고 문학이기 때문이지요.

사랑해요 명예의 영광보다 더 사랑해요,
미래의 영광보다 더.
나의 모국보다 당신을 사랑해요,
당신은 나의 고향이기 때문이지요.

당신은 귀찮아 하세요? 당신은 푸념이라도 있으신지요?
기도나 청원할 때는 하느님을 의심치 말라 하셨지요.
사랑해요 행복을 넘어. 정욕 보다도 당신을 사랑해요

# Я ЛЮБЛЮ ТЕБЯ БОЛЬШЕ ПРИРОДЫ

Yevgeny Yevtushenko

Я люблю тебя больше природы,
ибо ты, как природа сама.
Я люблю тебя больше свободы -
без тебя и свобода - тюрьма.

Я люблю тебя неосторожно,
словно пропасть, а не колею.
Я люблю тебя больше, чем можно -
больше, чем невозможно, люблю.

Я люблю безоглядно, бессрочно,
даже пьянствуя, даже грубя,
и уж больше себя - это точно! -
даже больше, чем просто тебя.

Я люблю тебя больше Шекспира,
больше всей на земле красоты, -
даже больше всей музыки мира,
ибо книга и музыка - ты.

Я люблю тебя больше, чем славу,
даже в будущие времена,
чем заржавленную державу,
ибо Родина - ты, не она.

Ты несчастна? Ты просишь участья?
Бога просьбами ты не гневи.
Я люблю тебя больше счастья.
Я люблю тебя больше любви.

## Sleep, My Beloved

YEVGENY YEVTUSHENKO

The salty spray glistens on the fence.
The wicket gate is bolted tight.
                                        And the sea,
smoking and heaving and scooping the dikes,
has sucked into itself the salty sun.
Sleep, my beloved...
                                don't torment my soul.
Already the mountains and the steppes are falling asleep,
and our lame dog,
                                shaggy and sleepy,
lies down and licks his salty chain.
And the branches are murmuring
                                        and the waves are trampling
and the dog and his day
                                are on the chain,
and I say to you, whispering
                                        and then half whispering
and then quite silently,
                                "Sleep, my beloved..."
Sleep, my beloved...
                                Forget that we quarreled.
Imagine –
        we are waking.
                                        Everything is new.
We are lying in the hay,
                                we sleepyheads.
                                                    Part of the dream

is the scent of sour cream, for somewhere below,
from the cellar.
Oh, how can I make you imagine all this,
you, so mistrustful?
Sleep, my beloved...
Smile in your dream.
Put away your tears.
Go and gather flowers
and wonder where to put them,
burying your face in them.
Are you muttering?
Tired, perhaps, of tossing?
Muffle yourself up in your dream
and wrap yourself in it.
In your dream you can do whatever you want to,
all that
we mutter about
if we don't sleep.
It's reckless not to sleep,
it's even a crime.
All
that is latent
cries out from the depths.
It is difficult for your eyes.
So much crowded in them.
It will be easier for them under closed eyelids.
Sleep, my beloved...
What is it that's making you sleepless?
Is it the roaring sea?
The begging of the trees?
Evil foreboding?

Someone's dishonesty?"

And maybe, not someone's

but simply my own?

Sleep, my beloved...

Nothing can be done about it.

But no,

I am innocent of that accusation.

Forgive me – do you hear!

Love me – do you hear!

Even if in your dream!

Even if in your dream!

Sleep, my beloved...

We are on the earth,

flying savagely along,

threatening to explode,

and we have to embrace

so we won't fall down,

and if we do fall –

we shall fall together.

Sleep, my beloved...

don't nurse a grudge.

Let dreams settle softly in your eyes.

It's so difficult to fall asleep on this earth!

And yet –

Do you hear, beloved?

Sleep.

And the branches are murmuring

and the waves are trampling

and the dog and his day

are on the chain,

and I say to you, whispering

and then half whispering

and then quite silently,

"Sleep, my beloved..."

*Translated by Geoffrey Dutton with Tina Tupikina-Glaessner (1964). Also published in Variety Crossing 4.*

## 님이여 단꿈을 꾸구려

**예브게니 예프뚜셴코**

소금의 물보라가 담벽에 부딪혀 반짝인다.
쪽문은 이미 단단히 잠겨 있다.
바다도
연기를 풀무질하며 제방을 무너트릴 듯이
이미 소금 해를 삼켜 버렸다.
님이여 단꿈을 꾸구려…
내 마음을 괴롭히지 마오.
벌써 산과 초원에는 어둠이 서리어 잠을 청하고.
다리 저는 텁수룩한 개도 잠에 취해,
소금에 젖은 체인을 핥고 있소.
쿵쿵대는 바다도,
쐬쏴 소리내는 나뭇가지도,
체인에 묶인 하루를 지낸 개도,
나도 당신에게 속삭이고,
조용한 목소리로 속삭인다오.
아무 말없이:
"님이여, 단꿈을 꾸구려…"
님이여 단꿈을 꾸구려…
우리사이에 불편한 것을 잊어버려라
잠시 상상 해 봐 –
우리는 깨어난다.
모든 것은 새롭다.
우리는 건초에 누어 있는
잠꾸러기
지하실에서 올라오는
마쪼니* 숨소리도

꿈의 한 장면이다.
오, 의심 많은 당신을
이 흥미진진한 것들을
어떻게 상상시킬 수 있을까?
님이여 단꿈을 꾸구려…
꿈에서라도 웃으면서
(울음을 거두시오!)
뜰에서 채집한 꽃 속에
얼굴을 묻으시오.
당신은 중얼댑니까?
고단해서 몸을 뒤척입니까?
꿈으로 감싸고,
꿈으로 두르시오.
그리고 꿈에서라도 많은 아름다운 옷들을 사시오.**
꿈에서 희망의 잠꼬대가
현실로 얼마든지 될 수 있다.
잠을 자지 않는 것은 무모한 일이오.
죄악이기도 하다.
마음속 깊이 숨어 있는
것들이 일어나 외치기 때문이다.
당신의 눈은 많은 것들이 흘러 넘쳐
피로하다.
눈을 감고 잠들면 수월 할 것이다.
님이여 단꿈을 꾸구려…
무엇이 방해 하는가?
고함치는 바다인가?
나쁜 예감인가?
나무의 속삭임인가?
그 어떤 이의 불신인가?
그것은 누구의 불신이 아니라,
자기 자신의 불신이 아닌가?

님이여 단꿈을 꾸구려…
이젠 할 수 없소.
그런데
내게 잘못이 없다는 것을 믿어주오.
꿈에서라도
꿈에서라도
용소해 주오 - - 내 말이 들려?
사랑해 주오 - 내 말이 들려?
님이여 단꿈을 꾸구려…
우리는 무섭게 비행하는
폭발할 지경에 있는 지구에 산다.
지구에서 떨어지지 않으려면,
포옹을 하여야 한다.
떨어진다면
우리 둘이서 함께 떨어지자.

님이여 단꿈을 꾸구려…
원망을 버리고
당신의 눈속에 보드라운 꿈을 담으시오.
이 세상은 안식할 곳이 못되잖소
그렇지만
님이여 내 말이 잘 들려? - 자구려…
쿵쿵대는 바다도,
쏴쏴 소리내는 나뭇가지도,
체인에 묶여 하루를 지낸 개도,
나도 당신에게 속삭이고,
조용한 목소리로 속삭인다오.
그리고 아무 말없이:
"님이여, 단꿈을 꾸구려…"

*마쪼니 – 구 소련코카사스 남쪽 지빙에서 생산되는 싸워 크림 종류
**러시아어 원문 번역.

*Translated by Dae-Tong Huh and Victor Aknine. Also published in Variety Crossing 4.*

## Tricksters

Barry Callaghan

"We all live with a lie
up our sleeve,
officers carry a leather wand
to make men disappear,
whole towns, villages.
Deception comes so easily,
we have changed wine
back to water again.
We are good at what we do.
Only the dove
refuses
to come out
of his hat."

*Also published in Variety Crossing 7.*

# 사기꾼

베리 칼라한

"소매치기하며
우린 모두 속이고 산다.
도시, 마을에서,
대리인은 요술 지팡이를 가지고
사람들을 사라지게 한다.
속임수는 이렇게 쉽게 흥행하며,
우리는 와인을 물로 바꾼다.
우린 이런일에 익숙하다.
비둘기만이 모자에서
나오길
거부한다."

*Translated by Dae-Tong Huh. Also published in Variety Crossing 7.*

# Hunger

Barry Callaghan

Surrounded by elms swollen with snow
our soldiers dug in during the December siege of '42
and ate cattle-cakes and boiled carpenter's glue
and froze to death in anti-tank ditches
refusing to cut ancestral trees for firewood.
"Children stared in their father's arms.
I die in yours,
You are someone from nowhere
I know nothing about."
A truck drove by half-loaded with drowsy pigs
followed by a skimming bird
pecking at ticks
plump with blood.
"When you undo my blouse you undo my bones,
like a king who sucks the toes
of his slaves,
you feed me your own hunger."

*Also published in Variety Crossing 7.*

# 기아

## 베리 칼라한

느릅나무에 소복히 쌓인 눈
42년 12월 아군은 공격시 방공호를 파고
가축사료와 목수 아교풀을 먹었다
대전차안에서 죽어가는 순간에도
불을 피우기 위해 조상의 나무를 자르길 꺼렸다.
"아이들은 아버지 팔에서 두리번 거렸다.
아이들아 나는 죽는다
알수없는 이곳
이 불쌍한 어린 것들아."
트럭은 돼지같이 실신한 장병들을  싣고 달렸다
썩은 조직을 추적하는 새들
부풀은 혈액을
순식간에 쪼아먹는다.
"나의 블라우스를 벗기고 나의 뼈를 제거하면,
노예의
발가락을 빠는 임금같이
너는 나에게 너의 굶주림을 먹인다."

*Translated by Dae-Tong Huh. Also published in Variey Crossing 7.*

# The Dazzle of Bronze Light from the Glittering Helmets

Priscila Uppal

Our mute Homers, is this how you see yourselves reflected
in an enemy's sunglasses, on the sour sands of fate,
uniform answers awaiting uniform suffering?

Do you see your boy's laughter in the glare? Or, like Hektor,
are you now unrecognizable even to yourself?
Where should we look to catch the light?

# 번쩍이는 헬멧에서 눈이부신 청동색

프리실라 우빨

무언의 호머스, 너는 적의 색안경에
굴절된 자신을 보는 것은, 운명의 냉습한 모래위에,
유니폼이 유니폼 수난을 기다리는 응답인가?

너는 섬광에서 아이의 웃음을 보는가? 아니면, 헥토처럼,
너는 현재 너의 자신까지 인식 불가능인가?
우리는 어디서 빛을 찾아야 하나?

# No Flags at Half-Mast

PRISCILA UPPAL

One day, when televisions are airing,
and veterans hands are to be shook,
the Prime Minister will pay for a wreath
of poppies out of his Mourning Fund.

Your mother and father will thank him,
because they won't know what else to do,
and they were brought up not to be rude, and
they want you to be remembered, belated or not.

We will have moved on to other, larger,
more prescient wars, and your boys' faces
will be reclassified "Safe" and
"A Tribute to All We Have Accomplished."

Today, however, the flags should be at half-mast,
for we are a nation suffering like doped animals,
half-caught in traps, half-hopeful
the man unhooking our legs is benevolent.

# 계양없는 반기半旗

프리실라 우 빨

어느날, 텔레비젼 공개토론에서,
노병이 손을 요동치니,
수상은 애도의 기금에서
양귀비 화환를 보낸다.

부모는 그에게 감사하며,
그에 어찌할지 몰라,
무례하지 않게 키웠다, 그들은
네가 기억하길 원한다, 늦건 말건..

우린 다른 사람에게, 더 큰 전쟁을
계속 할것이다. 아들의 얼굴은
재 분류한 "안전" 일 것이며,
"우리가 성취한 감사의 표시"일 것이다.

그러나 오늘은 깃발은 반기(半旗)의 위치에 있어야 한다.
마취된 동물처럼 나라의 재난을 막으려,
덫에 물린 반절, 절반의 희망
버팀대를 끄는 사람 자선적이다.

# Flowers

Anne Michaels

There's another skin inside my skin
that gathers to your touch, a lake to the light;
that looses its memory, its lost language
into your tongue,
erasing me into newness.
Just when the body thinks it knows
the ways of knowing itself,
this second skin continues to answer.

In the street – café chairs abandoned
on terraces, market stalls emptied
of their solid light,
though pavement still breathes
summer grapes and peaches.
Like the light of anything that grows
from this newly turned earth,
every tip of me gathers under your touch,
wind wrapping my dress around our legs,
your shirt twisting to flowers in my fists.

*Also published in Variety Crossing 6.*

# 사화 (詞華)

## 앤 마이클스

접촉이 묻히는 나의
피부안의 또 다른 피부 집결은, 빛의 호수;
서로의 기억을 풀어준다,
혀로 분실된 언어,
새로움으로 나를 지운다.
몸이 생각할 그 때가
생각을 이해하는 길이다,
제 2피부는 응답을 계속한다.

거리 테라스에 버린 카페 의자들,
우중충한
시장 축사에 작열하는 뙤약빛,
여름포도와 복숭아
포장 도로가엔 아직도 호흡하고 있지만.
생성하는 빛처럼
새롭게 도는 지구에서,
나의 각 끝이 너의 접촉에 집결,
우리다리 둘레로 나의 옷깃을 감싸는 바람,
나의 손안에 꽃으로 뒤틀리는 너의셔츠.

*Translated by Dae-Tong Huh. Also published in Variety Crossing 6.*

## 바다의 문 12

문효치

내 생애
비어 있는 자리,

물새 울음 한 조각
하얗게 걸려 흔들리고
때때로 빈 소라 껍질 위에
쓸쓸히 비 뿌려지는 곳

넓은 갯벌에
절름거리던 추억들
파도에 보듬겨 떠내려가고

깊은 병으로
아무도 모르게
타다가 타다가 재가 되는 곳.

# Door of Ocean 12

Hyo Chee Moon

In my life
An empty place

The waterfowl, a piece of her cry
Captured in pure white and shaken.
Sometimes on an empty conch-shell
The place of loneliness sprinkled with rain.

On the flat-mud
Hobbled memories
Drift away in a waves embrace

In serious illness
No one knows
The place turns to ash as it burns and burns.

*Translated by Dae-Tong Huh.*

## 공산성에 들꽃

문효치

이름을 붙이지 말아다오.
거추장스런 이름에 갇히기 보다는
그냥 이렇게
맑은 바람 속에 잠시 머물다가
아무도 모르게 사라지는 즐거움.

두꺼운 이름에 눌려
정말 내 모습이 일그러지기 보다는
하늘의 한 모서리를
조금 차지하고 서 있다가
흙으로 바스라져

내가 섰던 그자리
다시 하늘이 채워지면
거기 한 모금의 향기로 날아다닐 테니.
이름 붙이지 말아다오
한 송이 "자유"로 서 있고 싶을뿐.

# A wild flower at Gongsanseong

Hyo Chee Moon

Don't put a name on me.
Rather than confining in a burdensome name,
Just like this,
Stay shortly with a fresh wind,
The pleasure of disappearing when no one notices.

Weighted down by a heavy name
Rather than my presence truly being distorted
One corner of sky,
I occupy a little space, standing over there
Being crumbled to the earth

The place where I stood
If the sky fills in again
I will fly there in a single fragrant sip.
Don't put a name on me
I only wish to stand as a flower, as 'freedom.'

*Translated by Dae-Tong Huh.*

**Gongsanseong: Gongsanseong is a fortress in South Korea with historical and cultural richness. It is a fine example of a mountain castle from the Baekje period(234-678). It is located in Gongju-si region of Korea.*

## 비천(飛天)

문 효 치

어젯밤 내 꿈속에 들어오신
그 여인이 아니신가요.
안개가 장막처럼 드리워 있는
내 꿈의 문을 살며시 열고서
황새의 날개 밑에 고여 있는
따뜻한 바람같은 고운 옷을 입고

비어 있는 방같은 내 꿈 속에
스며들어오신 그분이 아니신가요.

달빛 한 가닥 잘라 피리를 만들고
하늘 한 자락 도려 현금을 만들던

그리하여 금빛 선율로 가득 채우면서,
돌아보고 웃고 또 보고 웃고 하던
여인이 아니신가요.

# A Celesitial Maiden

Hyo-Chee Moon

You came into my dream last night
You are that woman, aren't you.

The fog is hanging down like the curtain
From it opens the door of inside my dream softly,
In cherishing under the wing of a stork
As the warm wind, it puts on a fine cloth

Into my dream as the empty room
Soaks into it, wasn't that you.

With one piece of the moonlight it makes a flute,
With one edges of the sky it used to make a Gayageum*

By that, filling full in golden melody,
looked back and it laughed and also report laughing, it did
You are that woman, aren't you.

*Translated by Dae-Tong Huh.*
**Gayageum: a twelve-stringed Korean Harp*

# Sudden Harmony

George Fetherling

No incipience
but a sudden harmony.

Two figures in a
landscape
in a picture from
a text.

It's difficult
to choose the horizon
from among so many
planes.

The line ends at the point
where motion is set to
start.

Like a creature
hearing movement in
the underbrush
one waits in the rain
for the subtle change
in pitch.

Then the tide plays
arpeggios up and
down the beach.

*Also published in Variety Crossing 7.*

# 급격한 하모니

조지 웨더링

시초가 없는데
급격한 하모니다.

원본의 그림속에
조경의
2개 숫자.

여러
평면 사이에서
수평선을 선택하는것은

곤란하다.

선은 동작의
시작
점에서 끝낸다.

창조물이
숲속의 움직임 소리를
듣는 것과 같이
누군가 미묘한 변화를 위해
움추리고
비를 기다리는 것이다.

그때 조수는
해변에 왔다가 가는
화음을 노래한다.

*Translated by Dae-Tong Huh. Also published in Variety Crossing 7.*

## Notation 5

George Fetherling

The ocean takes its roar away
leaves foam in your mouth
and salt in your dreams

The pain is it there
but you don't feel

Shared of glass like snowflakes
no two ever the same

# 기호 5

조지 훼더링

바다는 외침을 잠 재우려
당신 입안에 거품을 남겨놓고
당신 꿈속에 소금을 남겨놓는다

일렁이는 아픔
깊이를 깨닫지 못 하리라

사금파리가 눈 싸라기 같은
둘은 결코 같지 않기에.

*Translated by Dae-Tong Huh.*

## 찬미의 강물

김남조

안다고 말하세요.
사랑이 그대에게 왔을 때처럼
속마음으로 말 하세요.
눈과 얼음의 들판에
꿈꾸는 연초록빛 어린 보리들
돌 틈에서 치솟는 청옥빛 샘물
설목 사이사이 불을 켜는 동백

깊이 안다고 말하세요.
가멸한 수평선 저 너머에서
바람 불며 바람불며
문앞에 와 계시는 손님
모두가 더운 가슴 한가운데에
물 긷는 두레박줄을 풀어 내리니
물 담아 올리느니

웬만큼 슬프거나 외로워봤자
삶에 보배스러움 보배스러움
굽이굽이 찬미의 강물이라고
말하세요.

# A River for Praise

Nham Cho Kim

Say that you know.
Like when love came to you,
Say it from inside your heart.
In the field of snow and ice,
Dreaming of young light green barley
Sapphire spring water streams between the rocks,
Camellia light up between the snow covered trees

Say that you know deeply.
Over there from an opulent horizon,
Wind blows wind blows.
A guest before the door,
All is warm in the core of the heart,
A line of the water-basket brought down
Lifting up the water.

Grief and loneness in small amounts
Is precious, precious in life
As a winding river for praise
Please say this.

*Translated by Dae-Tong Huh.*

## 조용한 시간

김남조

가장 고요할 때
한 음성 울린다
“내 마음 예 왔음을 그대 아는지”
“알도다 그먼저 내가 기다렸느니……”
나의 마음이 응답한다

눈나리는 새벽처럼
세상이 순백의 적멸로 완성되고
하늘 저너머의 어느 그 하늘인가에서
이름 없는 음악
처음 태어나는 선율이
참아온 온 세상의 눈물처럼
넘쳐흐른다

# A Silent Time

Nham Cho Kim

When most silent,
One voice rings—
"My heart is here, you know,"
"I know, I was waiting for you already….."
My heart answers back.

Like dawn with snow-falling,
The world is annihilated under pure snow
Music without a name
From a heaven, a sky above sky
Music without a name
The first melody is born
Like pent-up tears of the world
It is overflowing.

*Translated by Dae-Tong Huh.*

# The Boys Are Stepping Out Tonight

Joe Rosenblatt

As stars crouching in a summer sky
beam an eerie light on each earthly coat
drifting bands of vagabond cats coalesce
down in a ravine for a hunting orgy.
What nocturnal quarry do they fancy?
Are they after bunnies, deer mice, voles,
perchance . . . a creepy snake, or other feelers
without limbs who hug the belly of our earth
In any case, the boys are stepping out tonight.
The Fun King invites his monsters to a garden party
to be held inside a head that houses a brain
with no fixed address; but not to worry
dress is optional, so you can be your joyful selves
and yes, bring a friend, or two ---you can eat . . .

*Also published in Variety Crossing 6.*

# 오늘밤 사내아이들은 난동부리러 나간다

죠 로젼블래트

여름하늘에 몸을 웅쿠린 별처럼
세속외투에 쏘다지는 섬뜩한 빛
발광하는 고양이의 편류 악대에 함체한다
사냥의 탐익을 위해 계곡에 내려온 것이다
야간의 채석장에 그들의 몽상은 무엇인가?
토끼 다음에, 흰발생쥐, 들쥐,
어쩌면 소름끼치는 뱀, 또는 다른 더듬이들을
그들은 사냥하려는가
사지없이 지구의 아랫배를 껴 안으려
오늘밤 사내아이들은 난동부리러 나간다

농담 좋아하는 왕은 일정한 주소가 없는
지력의 머리 안에서 준비한
정원 파티에 괴물들을 초청한다; 그러나 염려치말라
드레스는 마음데로다, 너 자신이 만족스럽게 즐겨라
그렇지만, 친구 하나둘은 데려오렴 --- 네가 먹을 수 있게

*Translated by Dae-Tong Huh. Also published in Variety Crossing 6.*

# Sun dog

Joe Rosenblatt & Catherine Owen

To a crystal of diffracted ice
illuming a body beautiful, my spirit,
a dancing sun dog in the sky, conjoins
pulsing with another glowing lover.
My burnished pup, you have relinquished
the voiceless dark to yowl these rays
which shape a reliquary of our night
consigning my grief to a glint beyond auroras.

Deep within a ghost cocoon where souls pupate
and hum inside some twinkling kennel
vibrating their canticles to other stellar pups,
I caress your luminous pelt and yearn
for martyred Sebastian arrowed on earth;
his heart haloing the darkness.

*Also published in Variety Crossing 7.*

# 태양의 개

쇼 로젠부래트 & 캐서린 오운

회절된 아이스의 크리스탈에
동체를 조명하는 아름다운, 나의 영혼,
하늘에서 춤추는 아름다운 개,
또 다른 빛의 연인과 맥박을 결합한다.
광택의 강아지,너는 오로라 저쪽
섬광에 나의 슬픔을 건네주는
밤의 성물함
신음하는 광선에게 무언의 암흑을 포기했다.

넓이 용화하는 유령의 고치 깊이
반짝이는 개집에서 흘러 나오는 콧노래
다른 항성 강아지에게 그들의 찬송이 울려퍼진다,
나는 너의 명쾌한 움직임을 애무하고 동경한다
세속의 화살을 맞고 순교한 세바스찬을 위해;
그의 힘혼 암흑을 달무리한다.

*Translated by Dae-Tong Huh. Also published in Variety Crossing 7.*

# Pounce

Joe Rosenblatt & Catherine Owen

If you touch me you'll feel a surge of rage.
I have this urge to taste your blood, drive
my teeth into the shank of your ogling pity.
You turistas shall have no dominion over me.
I'm not your common street waif, I'm housed in pride!
My immaculate ears are the antennae of piety
for when the sun sets I'll bay at my master illumed
inside a burning bush on some sidewalk in Havana.

Ignore my Tudor hide, gristle lines my shadow, Che's
fierce love has sprung my posture. Not even perros
escape the virility of the imagination: I'm Cagney,
I'm Brando, I'm Capone! The heat swells my eyeballs
to fruit ripened in alleyways; I crouch over your grave,
Turista, the one the camera carves in your mind.

*Also published in Variety Crossing 7.*

# 발톱

**죠 로젠부래트 & 캐서린 오운**

네가 나를 만지면 거치른 파도를 만날 것이다.
너의 피을 맛보라는 충동이 일게되고, 너의
추파는 나를 유혹 할 것이다.
나는 거리의 여행자 나를 통제하지 못한다.
나는 거리에 방란자가 아닌 자랑스런 형상이니!
나의 깨끗한  귀는 경건한 안테나
하바나의 인도에 불타는 숲풀속에
나의 주인이 비치는 월계관 이거늘.

튜더(Tudor) 나의 은신처, 연골 선은 나의 그림자를 세운다,
무시 하지마라, 체(Che) 맹열한 사랑은 나의 자세이고. 개들까지도
상상의 사내다움을 피하지 못하는: 나는 캐근(Cagney)이니,
브랜도(Brando)이며, 캐폰(Capone)이잖니! 열은 나의 안구를
부풀게하고
옆 골목길 과일을 익게 한다; 너는 나의 두덤을 넘어온
여행자, 사진기가 너의 마음안에 굴절한다.

*Translated by Dae-Tong Huh. Also published in Variety Crossing 7.*

# Pouce Coupé

Robert Dickson

a letter perhaps to speak
of this and that the drought
and the fine weather and the wind
that rustles the leaves and shivers
my neck the travelling sky
two almost white draft horses
at temporary rest
a windmill figures as a bush-plane
with a brave and gluttonous propeller
the landscape dances lightly
under cartoon clouds
it's best to laugh a little
to the rhythm of the drums
nothing here goes faster than the horses
nor much more slowly
except the wind which takes
serious liberties the chill in the air
rolls down from the rockies
...

*the ruin of farmers solves no problem and makes many*
Wendell Berry

I
on the other side of the great big hill
it's work horses calm and dugout

work and peace

here i hear
a machine knocking down trees all
the trees such is the way
and the vocation of the machine: only noise
everything ripped from the earth and piled
on the ground and loaded on another
machine to be cut by another machine
to be sent over the great big sea to be sent
back in cardboard boxes as copies of
canadian antiques for vinyl houses
while the horses laid off await
the dog-food machines

here
my malaise grows swallows and larks
don't ease the apprehension a truck changes gears
going by close by on the highway
lines of gigantic machines are on their way
to extract from the earth riches for some
ruin for others money for roads and
machines progress growth of the gross
national product spending on fuel fro the machines
for the highways pre-cooked pre-learned
pre-cried and pre-laughed and life goes on
bustling and bewildering

on the other side of the great big hill
each bale of hay has its price
of sweat and survival

each horse is worth its living weight
nourishes the earth as it is nourished
works and rests pulls then rolls
in the grass where the greenness
is worth its weight in green

II

four belgians abreast advance on a hayfield
calm and diligent as this man
in august under an always uncertain present
soft sounds of harness summer birds and
squirrels in the alders along the creek
we will pick from the garden the evening meal
nothing bookish in this chosen life at
the fringe of the forest
this improbable love as luminous as
everyday hands
calloused washed in a minimum of water
it's not easy it goes
without saying nobody says it
it's no more (or less) bookish than a
prison where a man dreams of poetry
while deprived of working the land

another summer approaches its end
fall cleaning and equinox on the horizon
think about everything you must
so that all can be somehow just

...

*(from Humains Paysages — traductions anglaises)*

*Also published in Variety Crossing 5.*

## Pouce Coupé 마을

로버트 딕슨

이러저러한 내용의
편지 가뭄과 화창한
날씨 나뭇잎을 흔들며 내 목덜미를
휘감는 바람 여행해 가는 하늘
잠시 쉬어가는 두마리의
흰빛 복마 마치 변방 비행기처럼
힘차게 휘도는 풍차의 모습들—
그 풍경은 만화구름 아래서
가벼히 춤춘다
드럼의 리듬에 맞춰
슬쩍 웃는 것이 최상이다
여기에는 말(馬) 보다 빠른 것도 없고
느린 것도 없다
칼날의 차가운 대지가
자유를 쟁취하려 바람만
록키 산맥에서 굴러올 뿐이다.

농부들의 폐허는 문제의 해결이 아니고 많은 문제를 제기한다.
웬델 베리

I

거대한 언덕 저편 웅덩이에
조용히 누운 복마들을 보면
노동과 평온을 느낀다

나는 여기서 모든

나무를 절단하는
기계소리를 듣는다
기계의 사명: 요란한 소리
지상을 파헤쳐가며 땅에 쌓은
모든 것을 또 다른 기계의 절단을 위해
다른 기계에 실려 대양으로 실려
나가고 캐나다 골동품을 모방하여
카드보드 박스 안에 넣어
비닐 하우스로 보내고 있는데
은퇴한 말들은
개밥을 만드는 기계를 기다린다.

여기서
나의 불쾌감은 커진다 제비야 종달새야
나의 근심을 안심시키지 말라 고속도로에서
내 앞으로 지나가는 트럭이 기어를 바꾼다
땅 속에서 자원을 축출하여
자연을 파괴하려 거대한 차량들이
줄지어 달린다 고속도로를 위해
미리 계획된 자동차 연료를 위해
도로, 기계 발전과 국민 총생산 성장을
위해 돈을 쓴다 그래서 소란과
당황속에서 삶에 역사는 계속 이어진다

거대한 언덕 저편
건초단 마다 땀과 생존의
가치가 있다
말 한 마리도 생존의 무게 가치가 있다
땅에 거름을 준다 거름 주면서
일을 하고 쉰다
농기구를 당긴 후

초록이 초록의 무게 가치가 있는
푸른 잔디에 뒹군다

II

언제나 마구의 명랑하고
보드라운 울음이 들려 오는 팔월에
네 벨지안 복마가 사람처럼
조용히 열심히 건초 쌓인 들로
나란히 나아간다. 하구을 따라 오리나무 위에
여름새들과 다람쥐들을 본다
우리는 정원에서 저녁거리를 따 올 것이다
숲속 가에
선택된 삶에 독서할 필요가 없다
이 믿기 어려운 그리움은
극소량의 물로 매일 닦아
굳어진 손처럼 명백하다
아무도 말하지 않는다
참으로 어렵다
이것은 일꾸는 대지를
빼앗긴 사람이 시(詩)을 꿈꾸는
감방에서 독서를 하지 않는 것과 비 슷하다

또 다른 여름은 끝자락에 접혀오는
청명한 추분이 황혼에 물든다
이 때 삼라만상을 생각하면
다 그럴 것이다

*Translated by Dae-Tong Huh with Victor Aknine and Mina Cho.*
*Also published in Variety Crossing 5.*

# Pouce Coupé

Robert Dickson

III

if God played the banjo he'd be called
Béla Fleck joyous or melancholy
music would fill the warmth of the house

sun through the window above the sink
where I'm doing the morning dishes
glancing at the family garden
while the kettle sings a tune
on the still-warm woodstove

if he lived on the land
God would be small farmer
would produce pretty much everything
he could for his family
wouldn't be a multinational
wouldn't be called
Monsanto God
Cargill God
Agrobiz God
wouldn't practice genetic manipulation
his creation being complete replete
with inspiration
wouldn't play God
even though he is that and nothing less

wouldn't copyright the genetic code
of whole nations in truth
he has better things to do

and birches joining in a green
canopy above his head
the play of shade and light
through the green
and the harness leather and
the jingling and the blissful
smile on his weathered face for
work has borne its fruits and
there are these little moments
of tranquil joy
he'd bring in the hay with his
almost white horses along
the trail by the creek the alders
of extreme happiness
of eternity glimpsed through the trees

if he invited people over
on a Sunday afternoon
under a threatening sky
it would be these people
this wrinkled retired farmer
with the sound voice and
the obvious contentment
these incessantly chattering squirrels
this smiling woman singing
harmonies with her brother
pulling on the heart strings

eyes like a creek in summer flood
and these flowers when the sky clears
a full palette of colours right
into your eyes
and these little girls
jumping on each other and
rolling in the grass

these pines too
tall and night-green back-lit
the hand-made house nestle there
the campfire dances joyously of course
if he ate with his hands God
would have these same creases
at the corners of his mischievous
eyes these twenty-year-old stories
these jokes and the laughter peals
bodies shaking unabashedly

isn't it true he'd admire
all the simple things
the long day's work
the milk cow mooing
her heavy impatience
the dragonflies and the deer
jumping through the fields
sun on muscles and whip of wind
butterfly dances and bees in clover
he could read all the sometimes
funny stories in the clouds
but can't often take the time

coming back from morning chores

he'd warm up by the woodstove

perhaps with another mug of coffee

the kitchen full of the sweet smell
of peaches and apricots
planning for the long months ahead
the colours keep shining on
into the season of long nights
dancing still in what's left of the light

*(from Humains Paysages-traductions anglaises)*

*Also published in Variety Crossing 6.*

# 인간 풍경화- Pouce Coupé 마을

로버트 딕슨

III

신이 밴조을 분다면
벨라 플렉(Bla Fleck)을 연주 할 것인데
명랑하고 우울한 음악은
집안에 온기를 가득 채울 것이다

주전자가 아직 따스한 나무 난로위에서
자장가를 노래하는 동안
아침 설거지를 하고 있는
싱크대 창문을 내리비치는 해가
가족의 정원에서 눈짓한다

신이 땅에 산다면
신은 소농의 농부일 것이며
신은 갖가지 농산물을 생산하고
가족을 위해 일을 할 것이다
신은 몬토 신
카킬 신
아그로비즈 신이라고
불리지 않을 것이며
신은 유전자 조작을 실습지 않을 것이고
그의 창조는
영감으로 완전히 충만하여
유회를 하지 않을 것이며
비록 신이 유회를 한다 해도
유전자 코드의 저작권을 얻어내지 않을 것이고

진리 안에서 온 인류을 위해
신은 보다 좋은 일을 할 것이다

신은 그의 머리위에 오리나무와
자작나무들이
초록 카누피로 엉킨
실개천가의 길을 따라
흰 빛 도는 말들을
건초장에으로 데려올 것이고
초록색 명암의 놀이와
마구 가죽과
노동을 위해 탄생한 말의 풍화된 어굴에
벨소리와 축복된 미소의 결실의 모습에서
수목을 바라보며
고요한 기쁨
최고의 행복
영원을 바라보는 순간이 될 것이다

만일 신이 찌푸린 날씨
어느 일요일 오후
사람을 초대한다면
이들을 부르리라
건강한 음성에
만족의 충만으로
은퇴한 주름투성이
농부일 것이고
끊임없이 수다를 떠는 다람쥐들일 것이며
두 눈이 여름홍수에 넘실대는 실개천 처럼
심장의 현을 퉁기는 남동생과
조화를 이루는
노래하는 미소 짓는 여인이며

눈속에 비쳐오는
충만한 팔레트의 온전한 색깔의
하늘 빛 꽃들이며
잔디위에서 서로 뛰노는
소녀들일 것이다

키 크고 검푸른
소나무 역시 후광을 발산하고
손수 만든 집에
모닥불 역시 즐거워 춤을 추는 곳에서
신이 만일 손으로 음식을 먹는다면 신은
장난스런 연민의 눈으로
이들과 같은 주름투성이가 되어
이들의 20년 옛 이야기를 들으며
농담과 웃음로
태연하게 춤을 출 것이다

신은 모든 단순한 것을
동경하는 것이 사실이 아닐런가
오랜 하루의 일과
젖소의 울음
그녀의 무거운 인내심
들판을 뛰노는
잠자리와 사슴
내리쪼이는 햇살 거센 바람의 흥분
나비는 춤추고 클로버 잎 안에는 벌이 노닐고
그름떼 속에 재미나는 이야기들를 때로
신은 모두 읽을 수 있지만
수시로 시간을 내지 않을 것이다.

아침의 소일거리에서 돌아왔을 때

신은 장작 난로 가에서 몸을 데우리라
아마 또 다른 한 잔의 커피를 들 것이며
주방에는 복숭아와 살구의 향내로 가득 차고
아직 남은 불빛에 춤추는
색깔들이 깜박이는
긴 밤의 계절속에서
여러 달의 계획을 미리 짜고 있을 것이다.

*Translated by Dae-Tong Huh.*
*Also published in Variety Crossing 6.*

## Drunk Metaphysics
*after Ko Un*

Suji Kwock Kim

I've never been one soul.
Sixty trillion cells stagger
zigzag down the street,
laughing, trash-talking, quarreling,
singing-crying, living-dying.
Sixty trillion cells—all drunk!

*Also published in Variety Crossing 9.*

# 술취한 형이상학

## 고은 시인을 따라서

수지 곽 김

나는 한 영혼만 소유한 적이 없다.
60조의 세포들은 혈관에서
지그재그로 움직인다,
웃으면서, 실소하면서, 싸우며,
노래하고-울으면서, 생존과 죽음
60조의 세포-모두 술 취했다!

*Revised by Dae-Tong Huh. Korean translation by Seon Rai Huh.*
*Also published in Variety Crossing 9.*

## Skins

Suji Kwock Kim

Pretend I can't see
the lady in pearls mistaking me
for the kitchen help I could have been, or be.

Pretend I can't see
the busboy still working at seventy
bend over painfully.

Pretend I can't see
the maitred'
pretending not to see.

"Dare you see a Soul –at the White Heat?"
"Anger: anger's my meat."
"So I did sit and eat."

*Also published in Variety Crossing 6.*

# 피부

김 수지 곽

나는 모른척 가장한다
나를 부엌일 돌보는 사람으로
오해하는 진주의 숙녀, 아마 그렇겠지

나는 모른척 가장한다
버스소년 70년 굴곡넘어
아직도 괴롭게 일함을

나는 모른척 가장한다
보이지 않게 가장하는
호텔주인을

"너는 대담하게-백열에서-넋을 보았는가?"
"노기: 나는 고기에 화냈다."
"이렇게 나는 앉아 먹었다."

*Translated by Dae-Tong Huh. Also published in Variety Crossing 6.*

## 돌의 집

**박제천**

달이 뜨면 몸이 달라지네
아무리 뚜드려도
그 여자가 잠자는
돌의 문은
열리지 않네
돌의 결과 결 사이로
한밤내
달구어져 찍히는 내
손자국
아침이면
달의 무늬만
돌에 가득 차네

## House of stone

Je-Chun Park

When the moon rises, the body changes.
No matter how many times you knock
Where the woman is sleeping
The stone door,
Does not open.
In between layers of stones and stones
For all night long
Warmed up and left
My handprint
In the morning
Only the pattern of the moon
Filled in the stone.

*Translated by Dae-Tong Huh.*

# 무제

**박제천**

말하기보다 보여주기를 즐기시는 우리 하느님
사람으로 하여 뼛속 깊이 추워 떠는 날엔
못난놈 못난놈 하며
흰눈 내려 덮어주시네

말하기보다 들어주기를 즐기시는 우리 하느님
사람으로 하여 마음속 응혈이 지는 날엔
괜찮다 괜찮다 하며
비를 그어 가려주시네.

말하기보다 함께하기를 즐기시는 우리 하느님
사람으로 하여 마음이 따듯해지는 날엔
나 역시 고맙습니다
시를 지어 읽어드렸네

## No title

Je-Chun Park

Our God who enjoys showing instead of talking
A day when it chills to the bone because of people,
Poor, poor fellow, He says,
Then with white snow, He covers us.

Our God who enjoys listening instead of talking,
A day when grief falls into the heart because of people,
Okay, okay, He says,
Then with raindrops, He shelters us

Our God who enjoys gathering instead of talking,
A day when the heart warms because of people,
I also say thanks,
Then I wrote a poem and read it to Him.

## At Fifteen

Richard Teleky

Struggling with my French irregular verbs
I reached out through Daudet's Moulin
stories to a safe time in the future
when I could speak as easily as I read
and evening star looked really French
not only to that lonely shepherd who named
the royal constellations over the Luberon
but to me as well, the stars burned so hard,
for so long, their fires would never go out.
If I could reach back to that boy—touch
his shoulder, lead him on—would the future
have meant as much? Stars lead nowhere
                                        in particular.

# 15세에

## 리챠드 텔레키

불어의 불규칙 동사에 고민하고 있을지음
Daudet Moulin의 스토리가
나를 무난히 미래로 인도했다
내가 읽는 많큼 말 할 수 있었을때,
특히 불란서를 굽어보는 저녁별은 루베롱
마을위에 성좌라 이름한 고독한 양치는
목자뿐만 아니라 나에게도 응시 했다,
유난히 빛나는 별, 엉겁의 세월동안, 저 불꽃은
계속 되겠지. 내가 저녀석에게 도달할 수 있다면—그의
어깨를 두드리며, 안내한다면—미래는
의미 부여를 말해 올까? 별들은
아무데나 안내하지 않구나.
특별히

*Translated by Dae-Tong Huh.*

# Men without Gardens

Richard Teleky

follow blood,
rape and pillage.

This can be stopped
with an onion and a rose.

Two onions, two roses,
defy the bone-picker.

## 정원없는 남자

**리챠드 텔레키**

혈기로,
강간하고 약탈한다.

이것은 한 양파와 한 장미로
멈추어질 수 있다.

2개의 양파, 2송이의 장미는,
뼈를 쪼는 사람을 무시한다.

# Foreigners

Sonnet L'Abbe

Our first lesson is separation.

Men in one car, women in another,
We drive into unfamiliar.

I mistake an orum hill
For the mountain, until lifts
To reveal the horizon's true height. Halla

And Sea always facing, each other,
A proper old couple, silent,
Faithfully keeping to themselves.

Banners strung between pines
Coil in the wind, sling
Triplet fistful Hangul,
A stick and pebble alphabet.

Surrounded by this language
I cannot read, these strange letters
Are silk-swathed stones
That hit the eye without touching,
That leave a slow pain
But no bruises.

Only loneliness
The first lesson.

We speed into the wordless
Landscape.
Hurtling stasis, a year or two
Will pass like these first glimpses,
At the starling speed,
Of staying the same.

# 외국인

**쏘넷 라베**

첫째 교훈은 서로 떨어짐이다.

한차엔 남자, 다른 차엔 여자들이 타고,
우리는 생소한 곳을 향해 달린다.

고도의 수평선을 보기 위하여
산등성을 오르던 중
나는 오르막 언덕길을 잘못 들었다

한라산과 바다는 언제고 서로 응시하며,
침묵하는, 단정한 늙은 연인의 한쌍,
자신들의 위치를 성실하게 지키고 있고나.

소나무사이에 현수막들
바람에 감기며, 펄럭이는
손 서너배 크기의 한글,
지팡이와 자갈모양의 알파벳.

이 언어에 둘러쌓인다
읽을 수 없는, 생소한 글자들,
비단결에 감긴 보석
접촉없이 눈을 때린다.
아픔을 천천히 남겨놓고
그러나 상처는 없고나.
오직 외로움만이
처음경험하는 교훈이다.

진풍경속으로 속력을
낸다.
돌진하는 속도로, 1,2년은
우선 섬광처럼 달아나 겠지,
*찌르레기 속도로,
그렇게 체류하겠지.

*Translated by Dae-Tong Huh.*

*찌르레기 새: 인가 근처에 집을 짓고 살며 흉내를 잘 내는 새.

## Italia Mea Amore

Antonio D'Alfonso

They threw me out of my house,
they dragged me left and right,
from one room to another,
from one country to another.
They changed my name,
they cut the curls from my hair.
They laughed in my face
because I did not dress like them,
because I did not speak like them,
because I was neither white nor black.
They forced me to work
for a pay-cheque worth as much as spit.
They made me scrub washrooms
in factories, hospitals, cemeteries.
They raped my grandmother, my mother,
my sister, my daughter, my granddaughter.
They raped my father, my brother, my son.
They insured me, reassured me,
they fucked me good.
They put bread in my mouth
and told me I stole it.
They robbed me of my furniture,
money, job, wife and children.
They sent me to school
to learn the meaning of love, money and work,
They sent me to University
to learn how love, money and work were absurd.

They gave me a diploma
for losing my mother-tongue and history.
They taught me how to speak, swear,
study, steal, work, and think
in their language and history.
They took my meal away from me
and replaced it with bread and water.
They told me I was no one,
they told me I would find myself
in them by being like them.
They told me I was dead,
they told me you were dead,
they told me you were not mine.
They sold me drugs so I could forget
the colour of your eyes, the softness
of your skin, the warmth of your bosom.
They told me you were a whore,
a crook, a drunkard, an addict,
a hypocrite, a terrorist, a religious fanatic.
And when I called them the names
they had called you,
they spat in my face.
But it took just one look, one kiss,
one caress, one night beside you,
to rediscover myself
and understand what I am all about.
Now if they ask me my name,
I take the ink from your earth
and beside Antonio D'Alfonso
I sign Amore.

(*Montreal, September* 1, 1984)

# 外国人

赵 廉

在中国的时候，
我们把白种人
叫作“外国人”
他们来自西方
异国人的模样
有些自我恭维
多时过分客气
使中国人尴尬

我们又叫白种人
“大鼻子”，
并非贬低他们
这是国人的幽默感
和陌生人见面时
对他们超大的鼻子
表示特殊的尊重

但是，如果外国人是黑人
我们则说 “黑人”
而不是 “黑外国人”
他们的外籍似乎没有关系
当肤色成了明显的标志

1984年我来到加拿大的时候
我想这次该轮到我被人叫做“外国人”
在加拿大我是个外国留学生
我的社会保险卡是9字起头

可是没有人管我叫“外国人”
在加拿大，我是“中国人”
和成千上万的中国人一样
一个不多也不少的中国人

令我吃惊的是很多加拿大华人
称呼他们的白人邻居“外国人”或“鬼佬”
在自己的国土上，加拿大人怎么成了“外国人”？
不是这个意思，他们说，“外国人”就是非中国人

## Foreigners

Lien Chao

Back in China, we called Caucasians foreigners
wai guo ren, they came from the West
exotic-looking human species, self-congratulatory
their politeness embarrasses a lot of Chinese

sometimes we also called white foreigners
Big Nose, da bi zi, not in a derogatory manner
but a rather humorous way to meet strangers
by admiring their outstanding noses

but if it's black foreigners, we said, hei ren,
black persons, instead of hei wai guo ren,
as if their foreignness doesn't matter that much
when the colour of the skin becomes a definer

when I first came to Canada in 1984
I thought it's my turn to be called a foreigner
because I was a foreign student in Canada
my SIN card began with a digit 9

but nobody called me wai guo ren
in Canada, I am simply a Chinese
no more and certainly not less
like millions of other Chinese

to my greatest surprise, many Chinese in Canada

call their white neighbours, wai guo ren, or Gui Lao
how can Canadians be foreigners in their own country? I ask
No, that's not what it means, they say, it means non-Chinese

## Before I Die

Flavia Cosma

Before I die
I will speak to you about roads,
About stony hills with flowerless bosoms,
About the urge to run
And about desperation;
About lost wanderers—
The first of them, the last of them—
Or about those who are thinking to take to the road
one day.

Ashen faces, tired foreheads,
If one could only close their exhausted eyes!
The trembling lips, the demented whisper-
Started or not
All journeys
Descend into a terrible abyss.

Give me my life, give me back the jaunty step,
To reread them over like I would a book;
Somewhere on a bench
Under fragile question marks,
About departures that aren't departures
I will speak to you
Before I die.

# In Zilele când nu Scriu Poezie...

FLAVIA COSMA

In zilele când nu scriu poezie,
Mă joc de-a v-aţi-ascunselea cu soarele ;
El se strecoară ghiduş
Printre nori de hârtie,
Eu mă ridic pe vârfuri
Aşteptând,
Şi-atunci când vreau să plec, obosită,
El mă orbeşte râzând.

Când închid ochii
Sub pleoape zăresc picioarele-i de aur.
Săbii de foc taie zarea fâşii.
Ceasul bate rar, zilele trec cu greu,
Lumina se retrage sub pături ruginii,
Jocul de taină alunecă lin
Pe firul gândului meu.

Undeva mai la umbră,
Zâmbeşte Dumnezeu.

# The Season of Love

FLAVIA COSMA

Calm light
Early in the morning
Gently melts
The shadows of the night.

Objects, gray and blue forms,
Are jolted from sleep;
Substance returns to itself;
Daily life rises from the waves.

Imperfection recedes, yields;
Awed, we find ourselves again,
Complete and beautiful,
Filled with grace.

Peace surrounds us
With a grandmother's wings.
We reflect tenderly
On our fiercest enemies.
With willowy arms
We want to smooth their wrinkled, rough brows
And gather the tired, shortened flight
Into silky, silvery laps
Of the pious mornings
Of the young winter.

# Lumina lină

Flavia Cosma

Dimineaţa devreme
Topeşte uşor
Umbrele nopţii.

Contururi gri şi albastre,
Din somn obiecte tresar,
Substanţa revine în sine,
Viaţa diurnă apare din val.

Imperfecţiunea se trage-napoi,
Uimiţi, ne regăsim
Intregiţi şi frumoşi,
Plini de har.

Pacea ne-nconjoară
Cu aripi de bunică.
La cei mai vajnici duşmani
Gândim cu duioşie.
Vrem să le descreţim
Cutele aspre pe frunte
Şı zborul- nezbor, istovit,
Să-l adunăm cu braţul mlădios
In poala de mătase argintie
A dimineţilor cuvioase
De iarnă timpurie.

# Day of First Snowfall

Kijo Song

Let's meet the day of first snowfall
Red scarf wrapped around
Hope fresh in our hearts
Blowing on our cold hands
Let's meet and hold hands
On the afternoon of the first crunchy snowfall
When snowflakes roll down our frozen cheeks
And squeak under our feet
Let's meet and keep our body's warmth
Calming our nervous hearts

Let's share stories from old times
Place fiery love into the scattering snowflakes and step firmly on them
Blowing out words of love
As if tying the ends of clothes together
Let's look out onto the first snow falling outside the window

*Translated by Hyeamin Yoon.*

# БЫЛОЕ

Михаил Пак

Однажды
В детстве раннем
Услышал я звук.
Что это было?
Говор ручья ли,
Плеск облаков,
Шелест рассвета,
Плач листьев высокого тополя,
Шорох падающих звезд,
Ворчанье земли,
Прощальный крик птицы?
Не знаю.
Теперь всё позабыто.
Тропинка, ведущая вдаль,
Заросла высокой травой.
И сам горизонт подернут дымкой
Тумана.
Но всё же
В уголке моей памяти
Осталось видение -
Молодая женщина
Волосы моет в реке.
И слышится запах
Длинных блестящих волос,
Запах цветов полевых,
Осенних, буйных и терпких.

## Past

Mikhail Park

Once,
in my childhood,
I heard a sound
What was it?
Was it the murmur of a stream?
Or the spatter of clouds,
or the rustle of dawn,
or weeping of tall poplar leaves,
or the sound of falling stars?
Was it the grumbling of the Earth?
Or a bird's farewell cry?
I don't know.
I've forgotten everything.
The small path that led so far
is overgrown with thick grass.
And the horizon is hazy
in the mist.
Yet
I keep a vision
in a corner of my memory
A young woman
washing her hair in a river.
I hear the scent
of long and shining hair,
of autumn wildflowers,
luxuriant,
pungent.

*Translated by Victor Atknine*

# The Island (1)

Kyung Whan Yoo

White foam
surrounding the island

Revealing
toe-like promontories,

Watery loneliness
in between.

The island
is in our hearts

If we open our hearts
there is no island

*Translated by Dae-Tong Huh. Also published in Variety Crossing 5.*

## A Cape Jasmine

Kyung Whan Yoo

A great beauty
Hiding herself
Like a nun dress
Having a nobility in white
A Cape Jasmine

Its dimming and noble
Fragrance
Always
The body will tremble

The wide opened-petal closes in,
On a collected foundation
Spring frost that bites and makes you feel drunk
I want to have a kiss

It is its original nature
There is no need
To be ashamed.

*Translated by Dae-Tong Huh. Also published in Variety Crossing 7.*

# Song of May

Dae-Tong Huh

When forsythias sprout yellow lips
and green earlobes

and the crimson tongue of sunlight
brightens the pupils of your eyes

drops of dew that hang
on leaves
raise lanterns one by one

When I stand on the leaves
green voices are thick

Valleys, their waters sing clear
and even wild birds fly high

The folded wings
of my heart, too,
stretch out in song

# Nightgown, wife's gown

ROBERT SWARD

Where do people go when they go to sleep?
I envy them I want to go there too.
I am outside of them, married to them
Nightgown, wife's gown, women that you look at,
beside them—I knock on their shoulder blades
ask to be let in. It is forbidden.
But you are my wife, I say. There is no reply.
Arms around her, I caress her wings.

*Also published in Variety Crossing 5.*

# 잠옷, 아내의 잠옷

로버트 스와드

사람들은 잠이 올때 어디로 갈까?
나는 그들이 부럽다 나도 그곳으로 가고 싶다
그렇지 못한 나는 그들과 결혼 했다
잠옷, 아내의 잠옷, 내가 바라보는 여인들
곁에서 – 어깨부위를 두드려 본다
안에 들여보내 달라고 묻는다. 금지란다
당신은 내 아내이지 않소, 말 해보지만 대답이 없다.
팔로 그녀를 감싸며 그녀의 날개를 안는다.

*Translated by Hyeamin Yoon. Revised by Dae-Tong Huh.*
*Also published in Variety Crossing 5.*

# Laika, Dog Astronaut

Robert Sward

*The more time passes, the more I'm sorry....*
*We did not learn enough*
*from the mission to justify the death of the dog.*
--Russian scientist

"Dogs into cosmonauts.
'Muttnik' they called me.
And 'Laika.' The name means barker.
Bow wow, 2,570 times around the earth,
then burned up on re-entry.
Imagine me now alive. Comrade,
look in my eye. Tell me, what do you see?
Da! A dog biscuit 28 billion light years in diameter,
and it's floating in space. Luminous splendor
of the colorless light of emptiness.
That's the universe.
Bow wow, and you can hear it,
continuous song, the perfect but inaudible barking
of all the dogs that ever were.
Nyet, nyet!
God isn't done creating, my friend. God isn't done creating, my friend. The world is still coming into being."

*Also published in Variety Crossing 7.*

# 개 우주비행사, 라이카

로버트 스와드

날이 가면 갈수록, 더 유감스러운 것은...
라이카의 죽음을 판단 하기엔
우주비행에 대한 우리의 지식이 부족했었다.
--러시아 과학자

"개들이 러시아 비행사로 투입되었어요.
그들은 나를 '뭍닉'이라고 불러요.
그리고 '라이카.' 그 이름은 짖어대는
동물이라는 의미이지요.
멍멍, 2,570차례 지구 주변을 돌고 나면
재 진입시 불타버려요.
벗들이여, 지금 살아있는 나를 상상해봐요.
내 눈을 들여다봐요. 그리고 말해줘요, 그대가 무엇을 보는지를?
그래요! 직경 2백8십억 광년 속의
개 먹이 비스킷,
그리고 그 것은 우주에서 떠돌고 있네요. 허공의 무색 빛으로
빛나는 굉채.
그것이 우주랍니다.
멍멍, 그리고 당신은
멍멍대는 소리를 들을 수 있지요.
지속되는 노래, 완벽하나 모든 개들이 그랬듯이
알아들을 수 없는 개 짖는 소리.
아니야, 아니야! 신은 창조를 끝내지 않았어요, 친구여.
세상은 여전히 존재 속으로 빨려 들어가고 있네요."

*Translated by Mina Cho. Also published in Variety Crossing 7.*

## 파도, 바위섬

이길원

그 섬 하나
고개나 겨우 내민
바위섬 하나
가슴에 담지도 못하면서
어쩌자고
오늘도
저 혼자 애태우며
흔들리는가
파도여

## Wave, a rocky-island

Gil-Won Lee

The one island,
The head barely protrudes out,
One rocky island,
Even though it doesn't fill your heart,
For what reason
Even today
With self worry,
Why you shake,
Oh, waves!

*Translated by Dae-Tong Huh.*

# 강노을

이길원

강물이 타도록 노을이 고운 날엔
강가에 나아가 가슴을 열어보자
갈대 숲 그늘에서 물새가 나르면
노을 젖은 바람 가슴에 스며드네
흐르는 강물처럼 흘러가는 인생인데(삶이거늘)
강노을 바라보는 물새의 눈빛으로
노을을 등에 업고 흐르는 강물처럼
나 그리 흐르겠네 나 그리 살고 싶네

## River's Horizon

Gil-Won Lee

One day, on a horizon so beautiful that the river glows
Let's go to the riverside, and open our hearts.
When the waterfowl fly from the shade of the reed-forest,
The wet wind of the horizon soaks into the heart.
As life flows, as a river flows
Looking at the river horizon with waterfowl eyes,
Carrying the horizon on their back, like a flowing river,
I wish to flow in that way, and I wish to live as well.

*Translated by Dae-Tong Huh.*

# A Perfect Moment

Ashok Bhargava

In the morning
we were fire and sand.

Not sure who was who.

With a passionate glow
we melted and crystallized
into a rare and perfect glass.

Reflections of our dreams
beaming through this glass
made the whole world sparkle.

Like a kaleidoscope of
multi-colored marbles
we filled up the universe
with love and joy.

If ever I feel frail
the memory of this morning will
revitalize me.

# 완벽한 순간

아쏙 바그바

오늘 아침
우리는 불과 모래였습니다

누가 불이고 누가 모래였는지 나는 모릅니다

정열의 불꽃을 발하며
우리는
귀하고 완벽한 유리 결정체로 녹아들었습니다

유리를 뚫고 비쳐 나오는
우리 꿈의 반영으로
온 세상은 반짝였고

총천연색 구슬들로 만들어진
만화경처럼
우리의 사랑과 기쁨은
온천지를 가득 채웠습니다

행여 내가 약해질 때가 있다면
오늘 아침의 이 기억은
나에게 새로운 생기를 불어넣어 줄 것입니다.

# Words

Ashok Bhargava

We are our words
and words are emotions
Torn between the interpretations
of its true meanings.

Peering inside of me
I realize the impermanence of love
changeable and removable
with infinity on either side of it.

I wonder which side of me
really is me.

Words link us
my thoughts merge into yours
become one
bodies dissolve
poetry emerges.

Sometimes I am a stream
rushing to reach the ocean.

Sometimes I am a wave
eager to reach the shores.

Voiceless words vibrate against

the skin of our watery desires.

You ride the crests of my dreams
and dive into bottoms of the clouds
Where our souls meet and part.

## 말 (言語)

아쏙 바그바

말이란 그 사람의 반영이며
참 의미의 해석들 사이에서
갈팡질팡하는
감정들입니다

나의 내면을 들여다 보노라면
영원히 변하기 쉽고 삭제가 가능한 쪽
영원히 변하지 않고 삭제가 불가능한 쪽
두 면을 가진 사랑의 덧없음을 깨닫게 됩니다

진정한 나는
과연 어느쪽일까요.

말은 우리를 연결시켜 줍니다
나의 생각이 그대의 생각과 만나서
하나가 되고
두 육체는 용해되어
詩가 됩니다

때때로 나는
바다로 흘러가는 시냇물이며

때때로 나는
해변을 향해 달려가는 파도입니다

소리 없는 말들은

목타는 그대와 나의 열망으로 떱니다

그대는 내 꿈들의 정상을 날다가
우리의 영혼이 만나고 헤여지는
저 깊은 구름 층 아래로 뛰어드십니다.

# A Fling

Lilly Barnes

Leaving behind
the yammering of tasks
posted agenda
calendars and routes

Stepping off the path
of merits and accomplishments
of grim intent and expectations

I fling myself into the ocean of time

this shimmering moment.

*Also published in Variety Crossing 3.*

# 비우는 기쁨

## 릴리 반스

일상의 기다림
겹겹이 쌓인 메모지들
세월과 순례의 길
모두 떨쳐 버리고

공로와 성취
허위와 기대
길을 떠나서
시간의 바다 속으로 몸을 던진다

이 빛나는 순간이여

*Translated by Helen Kang. Also published in Variety Crossing 3.*

# Old woman by the well

Patria Rivera

It was sign of progress,
this artesian well
brought in by the Reparations Bill.
Portable water for the small, drought-stricken hamlet,
not rainwater caught in drums
nor shallow inground pumps
nor piped through dried-up mountain crevices.

This water would be good enough
to go with morning, noon and evening meals.
Water worth the wait
for barrio folk lining up from sun-up to sundown.

Resourceful middle-aged women,
mothers with young children,
waited for the overflow -
when in between pourings,
water was collected into a huge vat,
for washing dirty clothes,
for scrubbing unwashed children.

The week before the well's inauguration,
the lines of waiting women and children swelled,
the project yet to be finished,
the concrete yet to be poured,
the gears engaged.

The work crew proceeded with the test-run,
opening the spigot full blast,
letting the water gush,
carefully saved in tin pails, buckets, basins.

By late noon, the sun had hidden behind a cloud.
The line-up, too, seemed to thin
as an old woman with her bucket
took her turn at the spout. She barely noticed
her loose long hair catch the spokes
of the waterwheel. On the muddy ground,
dark-red squiggles flecked the runnels
of onrushing water.

*Also published in Variety Crossing 3.*

# Matandang babae sa may tabi ng balon

Patria Rivera

Ito ang palatandaan ng pagsulong:
Posong artesyanong
bigay ng Reparasyon.
Tubig para sa maliliit, natutuyot na mga nayon.
Hindi ulang tinipon sa dram
o galing sa mababababaw na mga bombang tubig
o sa mga bitak ng mga bundok.

Ito ay tubig na tamang-tama
sa agahan, tanghalian at hapunan.
Tubig na karapat-dapat sa mga taga-baryong
pumila mula sa pagsikat hanggang sa paglubog ng araw.

Mapamaraang mga babae,
mga nanay at mga anak
na nagsihintay sa umaapaw na tubig-balon
habang iniimis ang mga ligwak para sa
lalabhang maruruming damit,
kukuskusing marurusing na mga paslit.

Bago ang inugurasyon ng poso,
ang mga hilera ng mga babae at mga bata ay kumapal,
kahit ang proyekto ay hindi pa natatapos,
ang simento ay hindi pa ibinubuhos,
ang mga engranahe at mga ngipin ng gulong
ay hindi pa pinag-ugpung-ugpong.

Itinuloy ng mga piyon ang pagsubok sa poso.
Binatak ang piko,
pinabayaang tubig ay bumulwak,
matipon sa mga timba, balde, palanggana.

Nang tumanghali, nagtago ang araw sa ulap,
Umibsa rin ang hilerang naghihintay,
habang ang matandang babae
ay tumikad sa kanyang puwesto. Hindi namalayang
umikid ang lugay na buhok sa mga rayos ng gulog,
Doon sa putikan, itim-pula minantsahan
ang umaagos na tubig.

*Tagalog translation by author. Also published in Variety Crossing 3.*

# The Children as They Pass

BEN VICCARI

The wagon comes slowly by,
Grim, grey man at the wheel looking straight ahead.
Guard beside him, bludgeon face glowing with ale, rifle cradled and held like some obscene body part.

And in the open back, the children,
Dressed thinly, bodies hunched against the wind,
Some quietly sobbing, some mute.

The eyes of Miriam and Saul meet mine, Arms reach out to me as I am turned to stone
With only a silent scream to say goodbye.
The truck wheels fling pebbles to my bare feet that sting but cannot make me move.

They're headed for the train.

And then I wake and the nightmare begins again

# As Time Goes By

Ben Viccari

There is no steady march of time,
No inexorable tramping of burdened feet
As legions plod the Via Appia
Or Tommies slog it through Passchendael mud
Or the slow, silent erosion of an unholy matrimony
Or the fragmentations of flesh and bone
As cars explode outside embassies
There's only a whooooosh.........
From the cradle's wicker arms to the satin-lined casket and before and beyond, time continues

The space between my first and last moments.
Is an eyelid's flicker on the face of time

## Life as Dazzling May

Woo Sin Lee

Welcoming the yellow greetings of roadside dandelions while passing the streets
Strolling the park that was light green turning dark green
Looking at the cobalt sky and wishing for heaven
Coveting the artificial-looking red, yellow tulips in the cozy neighborhood flower bed
Planting apple, peach, pear, cherry trees in the backyard

Walking the flowered streets with a small pond of scattered pink leaves
Whooo ~ Blowing the cotton candy dandelion seeds with a puff of air
Counting the stars in the night sky, walking with my loved one showered in moonlight
Forgetting the night with the children, sharing thoughts at the coffee shop
Not tired even after staying up into the deep hours of the night

Oh, May is truly dazzling.

Treasuring the dazzling in my heart
Gathering the bright light so that
Although it may turn into gloomy autumn
Then into dreary winter,
I want to cherish the brilliance
So let me stay ever green

*Translated by Hyeamin Yoon.*

# Iron Wire's Silence

Choong Mo Jeung

When the iron wire is dyed by the morning sunlight on the bare mountain
Icy wind pierces through the barbed wire, separating the South and North
Stuffed, slanderous broadcasts are scattered like debris.

Although not a boundary, for over a century south and north
Still not able to get rid of the dichotomy of a single cell
Looking at each other while embracing the tragedy of separation

Whether white or red, only one and the same blood
When we are together as one race, we are able
But countrymen suffering hidden pain from the political fight

Vagabond nostalgia's wishing for the last
Despite helping many years
Is the north still filled with icy air?

*Translated by Hyeamin Yoon.*

## Tinged Autumn Leaves

Choong Mo Jeung

Autumn arrives with the bleak desolate wind
Seasonal birds cloaked with fiery colors
Ruffle their feathers at the rustling of fallen leaves

At every turn, sounds of winter rush past
Yet, why can't they disrobe their summer garments?
What do they yearn for that holds them back?

Quivering leaves on branches, barely clinging on
There you are, breathlessly panting
Emptying yourself makes easy that inescapable path

My friends, delight not at the sight of tinged autumn leaves
For the same sorrow emanates from a white-haired old man
A hundred years passes like a moment in a night's dream

If humans arrogantly fail to submit to
Nature's unfathomable laws, the Creator's Divine Providence
What can one say when facing God in the after life.

*English translation by Hyeamin Yoon. Also published in Variety Crossing 7.*

## Living Words

HYUNG BOK YOON

Absentmindedly spitted out words
lie dormant, without decay, under the shade of a tree.
After fluttering on the sail of the wind,
will push the earth out of its way as lettuce seeds sprout.

You'll see the seeds of the words that each and everyone has sown,
become rubber balloons in the yards of the neighbor's hearts
and fly up, up and away.

A small rose moss blossom's leaves that each one have nurtured.
Even when the leaves fall, the seeds become eyes to look up at the sky.
Life will chase the winged seeds
as it grabs clouds in the blue expanse of the sky.

This word, that word- all lump into fluffy cotton,
to climb this mountain, mingling with the towering mass of clouds
and cross that river.

When the words return after playing hide-and-seek between needle-leaf
trees
and knock on your ears one day,
Wide-eyed, you will be surprised
at how much the words have grown.

*Translated by Hyeamin Yoon.*

## Autumn

Eugene Huh

desolate lakes, home to spirits
steal warmth despite
fur, blankets, fire

blue on blue meets
diamond shoreline

standing amongst dry reeds
antlers still and quivering
loneliness watching

let me stay, in the cold clear
moment, the hard blue north desert

*Also published in Variety Crossing 5.*

# Wind Instrument

Adam Bohnet

The flute enchants the peg-legged centipede
To chase the silver-fishes in the hall
And wave his knobbed antenna at the wall;
Seduces Nike anarchists to bed
Techno-headed ravers on the floor
And turn Jehovah's Witness from the door.

*Also published in Variety Crossing 5.*

# Origami

Christopher Doda

In the room where you keep her
She works by candlelight,

Folding a piece of rice paper over and over
Onto itself.
When it is done
She looks up and hands you the weightless bauble,
An octahedron.

What is it?

It is your heart.

*Also published in Variety Crossing 6.*

# 종이 접기

크리스토퍼 도다

당신이 그녀와 같이 한 방
그녀는 촛불 옆에서 일한다.

얇은 종이 한 장을 계속해서
접는다.

완성 되었을 때
그녀는 너를 바라보며 그 가벼운 것을 건네준다.

무엇이지?

당신의 마음이야.

*Translated by Hyeamin Yoon. Revised by Dae-Tong Huh. Also published in Variety Crossing 6.*

# Earth, Air, Water, Fire

Charles Siedlecki

Earth, air, water and fire --
To what blind end did they aspire
When did, in accident combined,
Result in forming humankind?

Earth, water, fire and air --
What mystery was then laid bare
And to our senses, thus unlocked,
Whose answer was, by question, blocked?

What cosmic blunder gave us sense
To marvel at the elements
Of earth and fire, air and water,
To which we were both son and daughter?

We pray to gods devotedly
To claim their immortality,
Yet we arose from nothing higher
Than earth, air, water and fire.

*Also published in Variety Crossing 9.*

# Ziemia, Powietrze, Woda, Ogień

Charles Siedlecki

Ziemia, powietrze, woda i ogień -
Do jakiego ślepego końca dçżyły
Gdy naraz, przypadkowo związane,
Stworzyły człowieka?

Jaka tajemnica była wówczas odkryta
I do naszych zmysłów odemknieta,
Rozwiązaniem której była
Samym pytaniem, zamknieta?

Jaki błąd kosmiczny dał nam zmysł
Aby podziwiać żywioły ziemi i ognia,
Powietrza i wody,
Których staliśmy sie
I synem i córką?

Modlimy sie do bogów
Aby dosiągnąc
W ten sposób
Ich nieśmiertelność, a jednak,
Powstaliśmy z niczego innego
Niż z ziemi i powietrza,
Z wody i ognia.

*Polish translation by Author. Also published in Variety Crossing 9.*

# Dreamer's Rock
# A Place of Visions and Dreams

By Marion McGregor

High on the summit on Gwenbowensing Mountain, Whitefish River First Nation
Overlooking McGregor Bay, the Sweat Lodge and Rainbow Lodge
Is a Sacred Place of Visions and Dreams
On Dreamer's Rock.

Here the Ceremonial Rite of Passage takes place for the boys of twelve winters
To be initiated from youth to adulthood.
The youth lie in the rock depression on the peak of the sacred mountain
Each seeks their purpose on the path of life
Through their visions and dreams
On Dreamer's Rock.

The youth pray, meditate and beseech direction and guidance
From the Great Spirit and their Spirit Guides.
As they pray and meditate, they fast for four days and four nights
For inspiration and their souls to be filled with positive energy
During their visions and dreams
On Dreamer's Rock.

Facing the four directions in thanksgiving for their blessings, they offer tobacco
To summon their Spirit Guides.
The youth are not weak from hunger or thirst, for every sunrise they cleanse

Their minds and bodies using the Four Sacred Medicines
For their visions and dreams
On Dreamer's Rock.

The youth await their Spirit Guides to appear and announce
Whether they be a scout, messenger, warrior
Hunter, skilled trapper, fisherman, great leader,
Medicine man, seer or spiritual counselor
Through their visions and dreams
On Dreamer's Rock.

The Eagle as Messenger soars down, encircles the summit then returns to the sky
Taking the prayers of the vision seekers to the Creator.
The Spirit Counselors and Teachers appear in an apparition
To announce to the youth their purpose in life
During the visions and dreams
On Dreamer's Rock.

When their vision quest is over, the young men are enlightened about their purpose in life.
They climb down the summit on Gwenbowensing Mountain
From this sacred place of visions and dreams
Known as Dreamer's Rock.

*Note: Gwenbowensing is the original name of the mountain and does not translate into an English version – similar in principle to a sir name. Also published in Variety Crossing 9.*

# Enjibwaajigeng Waasehyaabendamowing minwaa Bwaajigewing

BY MARION MCGREGOR

Gchi shbaakaag Gwenbowensing aazhebekong, D'kmeg Ziibiing
Ekwa-debaamjgadek McGregor Wiikwed, Mdewgan wiigwaming miinwaa
Ngwaagan-gamkong
Enji Waasehyaabendamowing minwaa Bwaajigewing
Mampii sa Enjibwaajigeng

Miidash mampii shkinewenhsag nen-midaasiwe zhi-nishna boonigis-jig
naagadoowaad ntaawgiiwin
Wii zhiibaashkam-dmowaad waa-ni-niniwjig
Shkinweg zhngish-nook enji wiim-baapkaak gidaabkong
Ndwamdam-mowaad waazhi-naagdoowaad we-e-ne waazhi-bmaadziwaad
Enji Waasehyaabendamowin minwaa bwaajigewin
Mampii sa Enjibwaajigeng

Shkinweg namaawag, naanaagda-wen-da-mook miinwaa dash go-ge-goo
wii bgo-senda mowaad wii kinoo-maa-goozowaad
Dbgwaa-sen-damaan Gzhe-Mnidoon miinwaa Mno-jichag
Nadmaagenjin.
Shkinweg mkadekewok niiwgowan miinwaa niiw- wadbik.
Wii-moozhkeneshkwaad zhwenjgenwin miinwaa gwaash-kweziiwin
Enji Waasehyaabendamowin minwaa bwaajigewin
Mampii sa Enjibwaajigeng

Nii-wing nakeying nasmaagaabwe-wok miigwech wendamowaad mnwaa-
bne-ziwin
Semmaan bgitnaa-aan, wii man-dmaad Mno-Jigchag Nadmaagenjin.

Shkinwek bkwe-ne-dziwok en'so ekizhepbaawgag gye bkade-sii-wok
miinwaa gaasknaabaa-gwe-sii-wok
Wiimskwen-da-mo-waad miinwaa wiimshko-zii-waad.
Enji Waasehyaabendamowin minwaa Bwaajigewin
Mampii sa Enjibwaajigeng

Shkinwek baabii-yaahaan Mno-Jichag Nadmaagenjin wii bi-dizkowaad
Wii bwaachigowaad aanii-waaze-bmaadziwaad
Endgwenh E'kwaabid, Noodaagan, We-daasid,
Ntaa Giiysed, ntaa Dsoonh-naagned, ntaa Gii-goonhked, wii Gimaa-id
Wii mshkikininiwid, wii Jiiskiiwniniwid maage wii mkwa-dagoozid.
Enj Waasehyaabendamowin minwaa Bwaajigewin
Mampii sa Enjibwaajigeng

Mgizi, Noodaagan biwaanib-bza enj-shbaakaag miidash bskaapbizod
giizhgoong zhi-nik-kaying
Debendgjigenjin maajiidoowan namhewin.
Shkinwek waasehyaamdamok, Mno-jichag Nadmaagenjin waabmaa-aan.
Wiin-dmaagoowewziwin miin-nawok we-e-ne waazhnaa gdoowad
waanizheyaa'aad.
Epii-chi Waasehyaabendamowad minwaa bwaajigewad
Mampii sa Enjibwaajigeng

Miidash shkwa waasmowaabowad Kenjgenwin miin goweziwok aanii
waane zheyaa'aad.
Niisaakii-yaabkwa-sewok  Gwenbowensing aazhebekong,
Maapii sa enji waasehyaabendamowad minwaa bwaajigewad
Enjibwaajigeng teg.

*Ojibwe translation by Marion McGregor. Also published in Variety Crossing 9.*

## Shout

Helen Kang

One day I learned how to shout
and I yelled out as loudly as I could.
The shout went higher than sky and farther than the ocean.
They manoeuvred through the air like butterflies.
With them traveled my dreams and thoughts, and
the world unravelled before me.
I let my long raven hair in the wind;

I was free, and I was happy.

Then done day someone swallowed my shout:
A familiar, but it transformed upon hearing me yell
into an ugly Mouth that made me quiver with fear, and
with unforgiving teeth it shredded my shout into pieces.
I cried out louder, but Mouth was bigger;
The more I shouted the more silent I became.
I would have been better to keep quiet

So I did.

I listened in obedience to cruel Mouth
that ordered me to sit up straight,
that laughed at me for studying so hard,
that told me to get married rather than go to graduate school,
that reassured me that silence is a woman's way to happiness.

So I was silent.

*Also published in Variety Crossing 2.*

# Y la melancolía los traga

Kato Molinari

Uno entra,
uno sale,
uno entra,
uno sale.
El guerrero escribe:
-Todavía estamos lejos, en el piélago,
distantes de toda arista, de todo borde,
de toda incrustación.
Los hijos, en la casa de celuloide, piensan
que les tocó un padre demasiado raro, además del
desastre.
Y la melancolía los traga.

## And they are engulfed by melancholy

KATO MOLINARI

Someone comes in,
someone goes out,
someone comes in,
someone goes out.
The warrior writes:
-We are still far away, on the ocean,
far from any hill, any shore,
any incrustation.
The sons, in the celloloid house, think that
they were touched by to strange a father, as well as
the disaster.
And they are engulfed by melancholy.

*Translated by Brian Cole.*

# El are de la magia

Kato Molinari

En Santiago había un deán que tenía codicia de aprender el arte de la magia. Oyó decir que don Illán de Toledo la sabía más que ninguno, y fue a Toledo a buscarlo.

Jorge Luis Borges ("El brujo postergado")

El arte de la magia. De la magia que da permiso precario para escribir cartas de amor. A un pollo mojado. A un campesino. A un hombre que no tiene nada que ver conmigo todo que ver conmigo todo que hacer. Un hombre que me descubre, que empieza a mirarme. Un hombre que me olfatea. Un hombre que sufre su pesa de bronce en cada bolsillo. Un hombre que cuando se desvive por mi cuerpo sabe cómo sacudirse las pesas (en el suelo, lejos, asemejan gelatina prescindente). Un hombre.

# The Art of Magic

Kato Molinari

In Santiago there was a dean who longed to learn the art of magic.
He heard that Don Illán de Toledo knew this better than anyone, and
he went to Toledo to seek him out.

Jorge Luis Borges ("The neglected sorcerer")

The art of magic. Of that magic that gives precarious permission to write love letters. To a young man still wet behind the ears. To a peasant. To a man who has nothing to do but to see with me all that he sees with me all that he does. A man who discovers me, who begins to pay attention to me. A man who sniffs me out. A man who bears his weight in bronze in every pocket. A man who when he craves my body knows how to shake off the weights (on the ground, far away, they are like discarded jelly). A man.

*Translated by Brian Cole.*

## Sleepless Nights

MARIA PIA MARCHELLETTA

Sleepless Nights
Transport me
Into kingdoms of
Bitter sweet desires

Jewels hidden in
Catacombs of beloved
Dead souls of purgatory
Where golden glitter
Guides their dusty shadows

Selfishly I interrupt
Eternal repose
Insatiably seeking
Secret mysteries
With blindness, I ponder
To comprehend the
Unexplainable.

## Notti in bianco

Maria Pia Marchelletta

Notti in bianco
Mi conducono
In domini di
Desideri dolci ed amari

Gioielli nascosti in
Catacombe
Di anime del purgatorio
Di cari defunti
Dove una scintilla d'oro
Guida
Le loro ombre polverose

Io interrompo con egoismo
L'eterno riposo
Insaziabilmente
Cerco
Misteri segreti
Con cecità cerco
Di comprendere
L'inespiegabile.

*Italian translation by author.*

# Nuits Blanches

Maria Pia Marchelletta

Nuits blanches
Me conduisent
Dans royaume de
Désirs sucrés et amers

Bijoux cachés dans
Des ossuaires dans l'âme
Du purgatoire
De chèrs défunts
Où une splendeur d'or
Guide
L'ombre poussiéreuse

Egoïstement interrompt
Eternel repos
Avec un désir insatiable
Je vais à la recherche de
Mystères cachés
Avec cécité cherche
De comprendre
L'inexplicable

*French translation by author.*

# Essay

## Diversity — Our Distinct Advantage

By Dalton McGuinty, Premier

I've been asked to share my views on the advantages of multiculturalism. It's something I'm glad to do, especially with readers of this anthology who share my love for poetry and literature. It was Percy Bysshe Shelley who wrote: "Poetry is the record of the best and happiest moments of the happiest and best minds." It has certainly enriched my life and given me some of my happiest moments.

My father was a professor of Romantic poetry at Carleton University and he passed his deep appreciation for the beauty and spirit of poetry along to all 10 of his children.

I believe literature, poetry and prose are some of the finest tools we have to gain insight into the human condition. They provide a key to understanding one another and help us span different cultures, backgrounds, and even languages.

The more I learn about people, the more I understand that deep down, we are all the same, with the same basic hopes and fears. We want the same things — to live in peace and build a better life for our children.

Sometimes, I think we forget how much we have in common. We forget what ancient faiths have taught for centuries, and that is the basic truth about people, the one thing about all of us that is more important than anything else. It is not the colour of our skin, our nationality or our culture. It is not a matter if we are rich or poor. It is not about our ability or disabilities, our political systems, or our faith. The most important thing about people, what matters most, is our common humanity.

Here in Ontario, we live in a privileged society. Privileged in part because of our diversity. There is no question that our diversity is a tremendous asset. It fosters a wonderful view of the world — a world where we build bridges instead of walls, grow together instead of apart, and where there is no "us" and "them" — there's just us. It's a view that seems fundamental to building a strong, caring and cohesive society.

Diversity also strengthens our economy and our ability to compete in markets around the world. Together, we speak every language, embrace every culture and have ties to every market. But our diversity is more than an economic asset. It helps us understand that people everywhere are connected and that life is so much better for all of us when we support one another regardless of differences.

It helps us realize that the differences among people, whether they are racial, religious, political, tribal or ethnic, are not nearly as important as our common humanity. To me, this is the genius of Ontario and Canada.

Here, at the beginning of the 21st century, harmony and diversity are not just the path to peace, they're the link to prosperity. We are living in a time of declining birth rates and rapidly aging populations. Workforces are shrinking and skills shortages are growing.

Countries around the world are competing to bring the best, the brightest and the most skilled people to their shores. At the same time, the best and the brightest are looking for a safe, secure home where they can live in peace and prosperity, where they are free to be themselves without persecution, where respect for differences is the order of the day, and where opportunity is there for all, not just for a privileged few.

I'm proud to say Ontario is that place. This truly is the most diverse province in the best country in the world. We are where the world is going.

There is a global race to attract hard-working, talented, skilled people. The reward for finishing first is a high quality of life, because in today's world, knowledge and ideas are our most valuable resource. The great news is that we are a lap ahead in this race. We have a lead but it's not an overwhelming lead. I believe we can maintain our edge and generate the wealth we need to support our high quality of life. We can ensure Ontario is the place to be for years to come. But only if we continue to embrace our diversity and invest in the success of our people.

That is why we must strengthen our people — all of our people. We must do more than celebrate our diversity, we must embrace it and weave it into the fabric of our society. Because, when one of us succeeds, we all succeed, and none of us can succeed as well as all of us striving together.

*Also published in Variety Crossing 8.*

# 다양성은 - 명백한 장점

## 온타리오 주 수상, 달턴 맥퀸티

복합문화의 장점에 관하여 나의 의견을 나누어 주기를 의뢰해 왔습니다. 그것은 내가 좋아하는 시와 문학이 담겨있는 이 문예선집 (Variety Crossing)의 독자와 더불어 무언가, 나의 기쁨을 나누려 합니다. 퍼시 바이쉬 쉘리는 기고 하길,"시란 가장 만족스러운 마음의 절정이며 가장 만족한 순간의 기록이다."라고 했습니다. 시는 나의 삶을 풍요롭게 하며 또한 최대의 즐거운 순간을 앉겨다 줍니다.

나의 부친은 칼튼대학에서 낭만시를 가르치던 교수로서 시가 담고있는 아름다움과 영성에 관해 그의 열명의 자녀들에게 깊은 감상력을 물려 주었습니다.

문학, 시 및 산문은 우리 인간조건에서 식견을 얻어야 할 가장 아주 섬세한 도구라고 나는 믿습니다. 이것은 다른문화, 배경, 언어까지도 서로를 이해는데 우리에게 그 열쇠를 줍니다.

내가 사람들에 관해 더 많은 것을 배우고, 깊이 이해하면 할수록, 우리는 희망과 공포를 가지고 살아가는, 동일한 인간조건임을 이해하게 되며 우리는 다 같이 우리 자손들이 평화롭고 보다 좋은 삶을 영위하도록 기대합니다.

때론, 우리는 일반상식을 외면하고 살고 있지 않나 생각합니다. 우리는 여러세기 동안 가르쳐 왔던 선조의 신뢰를 잊어 버린듯 합니다. 이 신뢰는 인간에 관한 기본 진리이며, 우리모두에게 한가지 분명한 것은 신뢰는 무엇보다 중요하다는 것입니다. 그것은 피부색, 국적 또는 문화의 색깔이 아닙니다. 빈부의 문제를 떠나서. 우리의 능력과 무능력, 정치구조나, 혹은 신앙에 문제가 아닙니다. 인간배려에 가장 중요한 점은, 무엇이라해도, 우리의 일반적인 인간애에 있다 하겠습니다.

우리는 온타리오주, 특수사회에 살고 있습니다. 특수사회 의미는 다양성에 기인합니다. 다양성은 우리의 중요한 자산임을 의심할 여지가 없습니다. 그것은 세계의 흐름이며—세계는 벽 대신에 다리를 건설하고, 배타적이지 않으며 함께 성장하며 그 곳엔 "우리에게" "그들에게"란 것이 아닌 —우리뿐입니다. 그 의미는 힘, 친절함, 단결된 사회의 건설이 기본적인 것처럼 보입니다.

다양성은 또한 우리의 경제와 능력이 세계 시장을 점유케 하는 힘입니다.
같이서, 우리는 모든 언어를 구사하고, 모든 문화를 환영 함으로써 모든 시장을 연결하는 것입니다. 그러나 우리의 다양성은 경제적 재산보다 우선 합니다. 그것은
사람은 어디서나 연결되어 있다는 이해를 도와주며 이런 삶은 인종에 관계없이 서로의 존중이 우리모두를 위하여 유익합니다.

인종 상호간에 다른 점들이 우리를 도와줍니다. 인종, 종교, 정치, 부족이나 인종은, 우리의 일반적 인간애 만큼 중요하지 않습니다. 나에겐, 이러한 점이 온타리오주와 캐나다의 특징이라고 봅니다.

오늘, 21세기를 시작하면서, 조화와 다양성만이 평화의 길은 아닙니다. 그것은 번영과 연결됩니다. 출생이 감소하고 급속도로 노령인구가 증가하는 시기에 우리는 살고 있습니다. 노동인구는 수축되고 있으며 숙련공은 역부족임을 보입니다.

세계 국가는 가장 유능한, 수재들과 최고의 숙련 노동자를 유치하기위해서 치열한 경쟁을 벌리고 있습니다. 동시에, 최상의 기대는 안전을 이룩하는 것이며 국민이 보다 평화와 번영안에 살며 어디서든지 그들이 박해없이 자유로이 살 수 있는 나라, 일상의 질서에서 다른점을 존경하고 모두에게 기회를 주며, 몇몇을 위해 특권을 주지 않는 사회입니다.

나는 이러한 온타리오주가 자랑스럽습니다. 이는 진실로 세계어디에서 찾아볼 수 없는 다양성의 주 입니다. 우리는 세계가 열망하는 위치에 있습니다.

온 세계는 근면하고, 재능있는, 숙련공들을 유치하는데 경쟁합니다.
높은 삶의 질을 위한 첫번째 보상의 길은, 오늘의 세계를 관찰해 보면, 지식과 아이디어가 우리의 가장 귀중한 자원이라고 봅니다. 이토록 중요한 뉴스가 인종안에 겹쳐 있습니다. 우리는 이를 위하여

안내를 합니다. 그러나 강제로 안내하지 않습니다. 내가 믿기에는, 우리가 최상의 자리를 유지하고 삶의 질을 높이는데 필요한 부를 활성화는 것이 중요합니다. 우리는 온타리오가 장차 몇 년 안에 이를 성취하리라 믿습니다. 그러나 우리는 다양성을 적극 받아 들이면서 국민들의 성공에 계속 투자하는 것입니다.

이것이 우리가 인력자원을 강화 하자는 이유입니다—우리 모두가 다양성을 더욱 기념하며, 다양성을 받아 드리고 우리의 사회 구조안에 다양성을 엮어 나가야 합니다. 왜냐하면, 우리중 하나가 성공 할때, 우리는 모두 성공하며, 어느 누구도 함께 노력하면 성공할 수 있습니다.

*Korean translation by Dae-Tong Huh. Also published in Variety Crossing 8.*

## Importance of Poetry

David Macfarlane
*Author and columnist for Globe and Mail*

Thank you for inviting me to join in the celebration of the publication of Forum-21. It is an honour to be here.

I wanted to say a few words this evening about the importance of poetry. On such an occasio0n as this, before an audience such as you, it need hardly be said that poetry is important. By being here this evening, you have made it clear that you believe this to be so. Poetry is not only a celebration of language, it has the additional benefit of often being a celebration of particular culture. By this, I do not mean that poetry should be patriotic, or that it should act as an advertisement for any particular group of people. What I mean is that because poetry often allows us to see into the mind of the poet, it is a wonderful way of introducing people of one culture to people of another. If someone wanted to know something about Ireland, for instance, I would suggest that among other things they spend some time reading the poetry of William Butler Yeats or Seamus Heaney. If they wanted to know about Wales, I would say that they should go there, that they learn what they can about its history, but if they really wanted to get inside the mind of a Welshman perhaps they should read some of the poetry of Dylan Thomas. And likewise, if you come to Canada as a stranger, and want to know what goes on here, what should you do? Watch a hockey game? Certainly. Take a train across the country? That would help you understand how big the country is. Walk through the neighbourhoods of Toronto? You would then have some understanding of the many different kinds of people who live here. But I would also say to anyone who wants to glimpse inside the mind of the country that the poetry of Margaret Atwood, or Michael Ondaatje, or Anne Michaels, or Dionne Brand will help provide you with clear and intimate insights into this place.

I think of it a bit like travelling. Perhaps you have ha the experience of arriving in a strange place. You wander the streets; you visit the tourist sites; you attend concerts and art galleries. But if you area a tourist, you always feel – at least, I always feel – that you somehow can't quite get at the heart of things. You walk by houses in the evening, with the curtain drawn, and you think: what goes on in there? What are the people who live in this house really like? What are they talking about right now? Or you walk through the busy downtown streets, and you ask: who are all these people? Where do they come from? What are they doing? Where are they going? What troubles them? What gives them happiness? What do they believe?

As a tourist, you always feel that you are outside, trying to look in, but never quite succeeding. This is particularly true if there is a language barrier as well. I myself like to visit the little towns in the hills in Tuscany, in Italy, and as beautiful as these places are, as lovely as the ancient buildings and the views appear, what I always long for, as a traveller, is to be inside any-one of the little house I am passing. I want to be part of the life in that town, rather than a passing visitor. I want to go inside the little houses, sit at the tables, eat, drink, talk, learn. I want to get to the heart of things.

Poetry is a way to do that, so it seems to me. Reading poetry is like stepping directly inside the mind of someone – and so, directly inside the mind of that person's culture. It's as if the door of one of the little houses I'm walking by is suddenly thrown open, and I am ushered in to the dinner table, where everyone is talking and laughing and crying and telling stories. That's what poetry is. By reading poetry, I am suddenly at the heart of things.

It seems to me that this ability of poetry to usher us into new and unfamiliar worlds is especially important in a country such as Canada, and a city such as Toronto. We have Korean-Canadians, and Italian-Canadians, and Portugese-Canadians, and African-Canadians, and Russo-Canadians, and Chinese-Canadians. This great mix of people and ideas and customs (and food, let's not forget food!) is what makes Toronto such as exciting city. So much more exciting, believe me, than it was 30 years ago.

And yet... we do not know quite enough about one another. And not-knowing can mean, at the least serious level, that we simply don't enjoy one another as much as we should. At its most-serious level, not-knowing can give rise to bigotry and misunderstanding. So knowing one another is important – and poetry is one of the clearest and most direct ways we can get to know each other. It ushers us into the private worlds of individuals – and by so doing, into the soul of a culture. Poetry introduces us to worlds that we do not otherwise have access to.

For this reason, the publication of Forum-21 is to be applauded and celebrated. The efforts of the Baek-Ji Literary Club are to be commended. Literature is, of course, important simply because it is. Poetry doesn't have to teach us anything, really, other than how powerful beauty – the beauty of language, the beauty of ideas – can be. No great society has ever turned its back on the written word. In Canada, there is an auxiliary role for poetry, however. Quite an important one. As we undertake what is turning out to be one of the greatest multi-cultural experiments the world has ever seen, we would do well to pay attention to the poetry of the cultures that comprise this nation. For one very important reason – important when you are talking about a mix of different cultures, and races, and religions, and ideas. Poetry is always about understanding – and if understanding is one of the building blocks of Canada's 21$^{st}$ century, then we have reason to be optimistic about the country we are creating.

As a fellow writer – and as a fellow Canadian – I offer my sincere congratulations to Forum-21's editors and contributors. I hope we shall see a second edition soon.

*Also published in Variety Crossing 2.*

# 시(詩)의 중요성

**데이비드 맥팔레인,**

그로브앤메일 컬럼니스트 겸 작가

Forum-21의 출판 기념회에 저를 초청해 주신데 대하여 감사하며 아울러 영광으로 생각하는 바입니다. 본인은 오늘 저녁 시의 중요성에 관해서 몇 말씀 드리기로 했습니다.

오늘 저녁과 같은 경우, 여러분 앞에서 시가 중요하다느니 하는 말씀을 드리는게 좀 주제넘은 일이 아닌가 싶습니다. 오늘저녁 이렇게 모인 여러분들도 그렇게 믿고 있다는 것이지요.

시는 단순히 언어의 축제일 뿐만 아니라 때로는 어느 한 문화의 축제도 된다는 또 다른 이점을 가지고 있습니다. 이는 시가 반듯시 애국적이어야 한다거나 또는 어느 특정 집단을 위한 홍보 역활을 한다는 것은 아닙니다. 시는 독자로 하여금 시인의 마음속을 들려다 볼수 있게끔 하기 때문에, 한 문화권의 사람들을 다른 문화권 사람들에게 소개하는 훌륭한 기능을 한다는 것입니다.

가령 아일랜드에 관해 좀 알고 싶다면 무엇보다도 잠시 틈을 내어 윌리엄 버틀러 예이츠(William Butler Yeats)나 시이머스 히이니(Seamus Heaney)의 시를 읽어 보라고 권고 하고 싶습니다. 웨일즈에 대해 알고자 한다면 웨일즈에 직접 가서 그 역사를 배울수 있지만, 정말 웨일즈 사람들의 속마음을 알아보고 싶다면 디란 토머스(Dylan Thomas)의 시를 읽어야 한다는 것입니다. 이와 마찬가지로 여러분이 이방인으로 캐나다에 와서 어떤 일이 일어나고 있는지를 알고자 한다면 어떻게 해야 하겠습니까? 하키경기를 보아야 하겠습니까? 그럴 수도 있겠지요. 기차를 타고 대륙을 횡단하겠습니까? 그것도 이 나라가 얼마나 광대한지를 이해하는데 도움이 되겠지요. 토론토 시내를 돌아 다닌다든가? 그것도 이곳에는 얼마나 많은 다양한 인종들이 살고 있는지를 아는데는 다소 도움이 되겠습니다.

그러나 이 나라의 속 마음을 살피고자하는 분들에게는

역시 마가렛 애트우드(Margaret Atwood), 마이클 온다치(Michael Ondaatje), 앤 마이클스(Anne Michaels) 그리고 디온브랜드(Dionne Brand) 같은 시인들의 작품이 이곳을 분명하고 친밀하게 통찰하는데 도움을 줄 수 있을 것이라는 것을 말씀 드리겠습니다. 이것은 다소 여행과 비슷한 데가 있다고생각 합니다.

여러분은 낯선 곳에 가본 경험이 있을 것입니다. 거리를 거닐기도 하고, 관광지를 찾기도 하며, 음악회나 미술관 같은 곳에 가 보기도 할 것입니다. 그러나 여러분이 단순한

여행자라면 언제나 ㅡ 내 경우는 그렇습니다, ㅡ 어쩐지 알맹이를 보지 못한 것 같은 느낌을 가질 것입니다.

저녁때 커튼이 드리워진 집 앞뜰을 지나노라면, 안에서 무슨 일이 일어나고 있으며, 그 안에 사는 사람들은 어떤 사람들일까? 그리고 그들은 지금 무슨 대화를 나누고 있을까? 등등의 생각이 들것입니다. 그리고 빠쁜 도심지를 걸으면서는 이렇게 스스로 물을 수도 있을 것입니다. 저들은 누구이며, 어디서 왔고 무엇을 하며, 어디로 가는가? 그들의 어려움은 무엇이며 무엇이 그들을 행복하게 해 주고, 그들의 믿음은 무엇일까? 여행자로서 여러분은 언제나 밖에서 안을 들여다 보려고 하지만, 결코 마음대로 되지 않는다는 것을 느낄 것입니다.

거기에 언어의 장벽까지 있다면 특히 더 그렇구요.

나는 이태리 투스카니 지방의 언덕에 있는 작은 마을들을 좋아하는데, 그처럼 아름다운 고장과 멋있는 옛 건물들의 경치를 볼 때마다 언제나 여행자로서 내가 동경하는 것은 지나는 어느 조그만 집안에 들어가 보고 싶은 것입니다. 그저 지나가는 방문자가 아니라 그 마을에 들어가 살고 싶어지는 것이지요. 조그만 집에 들어가 이 테이블 저 테이블에 앉아, 먹고, 마시고, 이야기를 나누고, 배우고 싶어지는 것입니다. 알맹이를 얻고 싶다는 것이지요.

시는 바로 그런 일들을 할 수 있는 한가지 방법이 아닌가 싶습니다. 시를 읽는다는 것은 마치 어떤 사람의 마음속에 직접 들어가는 것과 같으며, 그래서 그 사람의 문화의 중심에 들어가는 것과 같다고 볼 수 있습니다. 그것은 마치 내가 지나치는 작은 집들

가운데 어느 한집의 문이 갑자기 열리고 내가 집안의 저녁 테이블로 안내되어 모두가 담소하고 떠들며 이야기를 하는 자리에 섞이는 것과 같다고 할 수 있습니다. 그것이 바로 '시'라는 것입니다.
시를 읽으므로서 나는 문득 사물의 핵심을 얻는 다는 것입니다.
우리를 새롭고 낯선 세계로 인도하는 이와 같은 시의 힘이 캐나다와 같은 나라, 토론토와 같은 도시에서는
중요한 것 같습니다.

이 곳에는 한국계 캐네디언을 비롯하여 이태리계 캐네디언, 포르투갈계 캐네디언, 아프리카계 캐네디언 그리고 러시아계 캐네디언과 중국계 캐네디언들이 살고 있습니다.
이처럼 매우 다양한 민족사상 관습(음식을 잊지 맙시다)의 혼합이 토론토을 이렇게 재미있는 도시로 만들고 있는 것입니다. 30 년전보다 엄청나게 재미있는 도시가 되고
있음을 믿으십시요.

그럼에도 우리는 서로를 잘 모르고 있습니다. 그리고 서로를 잘 모른다는 것은, 다소 너그럽게 보아서 마땅히 그러해야만 하는데도 서로 간에 즐거움을 나누지 못한다는 것이지요. 좀 지나치게 말한다면 잘 모른다는 것은 편협과 오해를 불러 일으킬 수 있다는 사실입니다.
그만큼 상대방을 안다는 것은 중요한 일이며, 시가 바로 우리가 서로를 알 수 있는 가장 분명하고, 가장 직접적인 방법의 하나인 것입니다. 시는 각 개인의 사사로운 세계로 우리를 인도하며, 동시에 한 문화의 영혼속으로 우리를 인도하는 것입니다.
시는 다른 방법으로 접근할 수 없는 여러 세계를 우리들에게 소개하는 것이지요.

이와 같은 이유로 Forum-21의 출간은 갈채와 축하를 받아야 합니다.
백지문학회의 노력은 마땅히 치하를 받아야 합니다. 물론 문학은 단순히 문학이라는 이유만으로도 중요합니다. 시는 사실 우리에게 무엇인가를 가르쳐야만 되는 것은 아닙니다.
얼마나 강력한 아름다움 — 언어의 아름다움, 사고의 아름다움 — 이 될 수 있는가 하는 것뿐입니다.

훌륭한 사회치고 기록된 언어에 등을 돌리는 일은 없습니다. 그런데 캐나다에는 시를 위한 또 다른 역활이 있습니다. 매우 중요한 역활이지요.

우리는 세계에서 유례없는 귀중한 복합문화를 실험하고 있는 중이므로 이 국가를 구성하고 있는 문화의 시에 각별한 관심을 가져야 할 것입니다. 여러분이 혼합된 다른 문화와 민족, 종교와 사상 등에 관해 이야기할 때 시가 중요하다는 것입니다.

시는 언제나 이해에 관한 것입니다. 그리고 만약 이 이해가 캐나다의 21세기를 건설하는 건축자재의 하나라면 우리는 우리가 창조해가는 국가에 대해 낙관할 수 있는 이유를 가지고 있는 셈입니다. 같은 문필가의 한 사람으로서, 그리고 캐나다 동포의 한 사람으로서 Forum-21의 편집인과 기고자 여러분들께 진심으로 축하의 말씀을 드립니다.

머지않아 제 2집을 볼 수 있게 되기를 바랍니다.

*Translated by Dae-Tong Huh. Also published in Variety Crossing 2.*

# Congratulations

DAVID MACFARLANE

I would like to take this opportunity to congratulate everyone involved in the publication of the $5^{th}$ volume of Variety Crossing. This is a remarkable achievement. It should be cause for great celebration – partly because poetry and good writing is always cause for celebration, but also because this is exactly the kind of cultural project that makes living in a city such as Toronto so exciting.

At the launch of the 1st volume of Variety Crossing, I pointed out that poetry is a particularly appropriate kind of writing for the Korean-Canadian community to highlight in a multi-cultural metropolis such as this. I feel all the more strongly about the writing featured in this new collection. Not because I am familiar it, or because I understand it completely. (Good writing, I think always leaves something at the edges isn't quite understood.) No, my reason for congratulating the Korean-Canadian Literary Forum-21 on their persistence and in their dedication, is that writing provides us with an intimate view of one another's communities that we might not otherwise have.

I compared living in a city such as Toronto – with its Korean neighbourhoods: its Chinese, its Greek, its Italian, its Portuguese, its Indian and Pakistani, its Russian and Vietnamese – with visiting another country. Often, as a tourist, I have wondered the streets of some great city, and have peered into the windows of the houses I pass. I always feel that as wonderful as it is to be visiting a new place, what I really want to know is what goes on behind those windows.

Our city is often much like this. We see one another and, thankfully, for the most part, we respect and enjoy one another's presence. But sadly perhaps, we do not know one another as intimately as we should. We do not really know what goes on behind those windows that we pass.

The publication of Variety Crossing is an invitation to look inside the windows of a culture that we who are not of it, respect and admire, but do not know as well as we should. Writing is often very intimate. It is emotional. It is revealing. Sometimes it's shocking or disturbing, sometimes funny, and joyous. These are the things that are visible to people when they are allowed to look in through the windows. They learn things. They understand things. They become aware.

This is enormously important – particularly in a city such as Toronto. The equation is quite simple: the more we know of one another, the more understanding we are. But there's something else, too: it's not only a matter of keeping peace between communities. The more we know one another, the richer we are. Our culture is always the better for knowing other cultures – and, if possible, for knowing them intimately. For this reason, more than any other, we can only be grateful for Variety Crossing.

Congratulations.

*Also published in Variety Crossing 5.*

# Market backs fruits of poet's labour
# Dae Tong Huh wanted to share life experiences

JOE FIORITO
*Author / Columnist for The National Post*

In the morning, before he opens the doors of his corner store, Dae Tong Huh hops in his van and heads across town to the Ontario Food Terminal to pick up the day's supplies. Dae Tong is officially retired. The store belongs to his wife. He does her bidding. "She's a real slave-driver," he smiles, making a careful left turn. The air is cool, the light is clean, traffic is gentle at this hour. Dae Tong Huh is a man who is happy to do his wife's bidding.

At the Ontario Food Terminal, he finds a narrow parking space, buys a cup of coffee, and takes a stroll. He needs to stock up on fresh flowers – people in the Annex buy a lot of flowers. "Look at these. Nice begonias, very good colour. And garden mums – you plant them this year, they will come back the next." He selects one flat of brilliant red begonias, three big pots of mums, and a couple of buckets of showy little sunflowers.

When the deal's done and his flowers are stowed in the back of the van, Dae Tong takes his pleasure strolling amid the aisles of bushel baskets bulging with the splendid produce of Ontario in August – tomatoes and cranberry beans, fresh berries, blushing peaches and purple onions, green peppers and red lettuce.

Everyone here knows Dae Tong. And, it seems most of the suppliers at the Ontario Food Terminal have invested in him.

I don't mean they have invested in a little corner store on the other side of town. They have put their money on Dae Tong Huh, Korean-Canadian poet, president of the Ko-Can Literary Club, and editor of the soon-to-be launched second edition of a bilingual, multicultural literary journal, Variety Crossing.

Over a plate of Food Terminal sausage and eggs, Dae Tong Huh tells me the story, start to finish.

After his father died in the Korean war, he immigrated to the United States. He came to Toronto in 1969 and got a job in the lab of a local hospital. He worked hard, brought his five brothers and his sister over from Korea, raised a family of his own, put in his 20 years at the hospital, and then retired.

He helped out in the store.

And did his wife's bidding.

But, with time on his hand, he began to think about the big issues. Life and death. The nature of identity. The meaning of culture. He joined a couple of choirs – he's a tenor – and began to study voice at the Royal Conservatory.

"I have had a variety experiences in my life – war and hunger, I was singing in my choirs and doing woodcarving, but it was not enough. My experiences wanted to come out."

They eventually came out in the form of poems; poetry led him to quit the choirs and join a small group of Korean-Canadian writers, of which he is president this year.

There isn't much point in writing if nobody reads what's written. Hence the anthology. As these things go, Variety Crossing is modest in size and grand in ambition – its goal is nothing less than the bridging of cultures and traditions.

But it costs money to publish a literary journal. The Ko-Can Literary Club is not exactly awash in cash. Dae Tong Huh is not rich. He is, however, charming, determined and resourceful. He approached the people he knows best – the flower and fruit suppliers at the Ontario Food Terminal – and asked them for donations.

"Everywhere in the world, you find farmers are the most gentle people." Not to mention the most generous. At least 20 growers and suppliers responded with small amounts of money, based on faith and friendship.

Variety Crossing could not have been published without them. It contains the work of 11 writers of various ethnic backgrounds. It is published in Korean and English. And it will be launched on September 10, from 7-10 p.m., at Rowers' Pub, 150 Harbord St.

*This article originally appeared in The National Post on August 24, 2000.*
*Also published in Variety Crossing 2.*

# 시인의 노력의 결실을 후원해 주는 시장

## —삶에 체험을 나누기를 원하는 허대통씨—

조 피어리토, 내셔날 포스트 커럼니스트

이른 아침, 그는 가게를 열기전 벤에 올라 시가지를 가로질러 그날 필요한 물건을 사기 위하여 청과업시장으로 향한다. 대통은 공식적으로 은퇴했다. 가게는 그의 아내의 소유다. 그는 아내의 명령에 따른다. "그녀는 나를 종처럼 부린단 말야" 말을 던지며 조심스럽게 좌회전을 하면서 빙긋이 웃는다. 서늘한 아침공기, 맑게 비치는 햇빛, 교통체증도 이 시간엔 한가하다. 대통은 아내의 요구대로 일하는 행복한 남편이다.

그는 청과업시장에 도착해서 좁다란 주차공간에 벤을 세우고는 커피 한 잔을 사들고 주위를 살피며 걷는다. 필요한 만큼 신선한 꽃을 사기 위해서다 — 아넥스 주민들이 꽃을 사기 때문이다. "자 꽃들을 좀 보시오. 섬세한 베고니아, 매우 아름다운 색깔이지요. 또한 정원에 심는 국화들을 보세요 — 금년에 심으면 내년에도 피지요." 그는 눈이 부시는 붉은 베고니아, 세 개의 큰 화분 국화, 그리고 한 바스켓의 작은 해바라기를 샀다. 계산을 끝낸 후 꽃들을 벤 뒤에 싣고, 대통은 8월이면 이곳 온타리오주에서 풍성히 생산되는 각종 과일, 채소가 가득 넘쳐 흐르는 부셀 바구니 사이를 즐거운 마음으로 걷는다 — 토마토와 크렌베리 딸기, 얼굴처럼 붉은 빛깔의 복숭아와 자주빛 양파, 녹색의 후추와 붉은 상추의 부셀들. 대부분 여기서 만나는 이들은 대통을 안다. 마치 온타리오 청과업 시장의 대부분의 공급자들이 대통에게 투자하는것 같다.

내가 말하고자 하는 것은 그들이 도시주변에 있는 한 작은 코너의 가게에 투자하자는 것이 아니다. 그들은 한카 시인이며, 한카문학동호인회 회장인 대통씨에게 그들의 돈을 기증 했다는 것이다. 곧 출간되는 이중언어와 복합 문예지로 불리우는 제 2집 버라이어티 크로싱(다양성의 만남) 편집인이기도 한 대통씨에게 투자하는 것이다.

청과업 식당에 올라와 소세지와 계란이 풍성하게 담긴 접시를 응시하며 대통씨는 필자에게 자신에 대해 소상하게 말을 꺼낸다.
지난 한국전에서 부친을 잃었고 그는 미국유학을 거쳐 69년 토론토에 이주 병원 실험실에 일자리를 얻었다. 그는 열심히 일하면서, 한국에 있는 5명의 형제와 여동생 가족들을 캐나다에 이민 시켰으며, 자신의 가족을 부양하면서 20년 넘게 병원에서 일한 후 일찍 퇴직했다.
그는 가게 일들을 도우며, 아내가 필요한 물건을 구입해 오기도 한다.
이 와중에도, 시간이 주어질 때면, 그는 중요한 문제에 관해 사색하기 시작한다. 죽음과 삶에 관해서,
자연의 속성의 문제며 문화의 의미에 관해서 등.

로열콘서버토리에서 성악공부를 시작 그는 합창단에 테네멤버로 가입했다.

"나는 여러가지 인생을 체험했습니다 — 전쟁의 슬픔과 기아의 절망, 합창단에서 노래하고, 목각을 해 보았지만, 이런 것들은 나의 내심의 욕구를 충족시키지 못했습니다. 나의 삶에 사색들은 끈질기게 분출해 나오기를 원하고 있었지요."

이것들은 궁국적으로 시의 형태로 표출 되었고 — 시성은 그로 하여금합창단을 떠나게 했으며 작은 한카문인단체에 가입하도록 인도했다. 그는 현재 한카문학동호인회 회장이다.

아무리 작품을 썼다해도 독자가 없으면 작품의 가치가 없다.
이에 따른 작품 선집으로 이를 감안한 문예지, 버라어티 크로싱은 적당한 크기에 큰 뜻이 담겨있다— 기같은 대망은 서로 다른 문화들의 교량 역할을 통해 고유한 캐나다의 전통을 창조하는 것이다.

그러나 이문예지를 출판하기 위하여는 상당한 자금이 필요하다.
한카문학동호인회는 이만한 재산이 없었고 대통 역시 부자가 아니다.
그렇지만, 그는 매력적이고
결단력이 있으며 재주있는 사람이다. 그는 그가 평상시에 잘 알고 있는 삶들을 접촉했다— 그는 온타리오 청과시장에서 꽃과 채소를 재배하는 공급자들을 접근하여—기부금을 받어낸 것이다.

"이 세상 어디서도, 당신은 대부분 농부들은 진실한 사람들이란 것을 알것이요."

그렇다고 이들 대다수가 기부금을 주는데 관하다는 것은 아니다. 20명 가량의 꽃 재배자들과 공급자들의 도움이 있었는데—그들은 평상시 신의와 우정을 나누던 사람들이었다.

버라이어티 크로싱은 이들의 도움이 없이는 불가능 했었다. 이 문예지는 다양한 인종문화의 배경을 이루는 11명의 작가들의 글을 담고 있다. 오는 9월 10일 하보드 150번지에 위치한 로워스 팝 주점에서 출판 기념회을 갖는다.

*This article originally appeared in The National Post on August 24, 2000.*

*Translated by Dae-Tong Huh. Also published in Variety Crossing 3.*

# Consciousness Loves Contrast: Multicultural Creativity

PAUL SALTZMAN
*Film director, producer*

Good evening, Ladies and Gentlemen. It is truly an honour and a delight to be here with you. It is an honour because the Baek-Ji Literary Club has included two short poems of mine in their first Forum-21 book; and it's a delight for this is the first time my poetry has been published.

However, it is even more delightful because I feel my world has expanded. My life is truly enriched by sharing this celebration with you, and by having met Kyoung Soon and Dae-Tong Huh, as well as Mr. Nahm and Mr. Choi. I'd like to explain this.

I'm a filmmaker by profession. I started working in television and film in 1965 and since then I've directed or produced 240 dramas and about 60 documentaries. And even though I've had many pleasures over the past 35 years, like meeting Robert Redford ... hugging Audrey Hepburn ... winning two Emmy Awards and many other film awards, the greatest pleasure I've had as a filmmaker was making a series of 26 documentaries, which we filmed in 22 countries, on creativity in young people and the passing down of creative traditions from one generation to the next, in different cultures.

In each case, as I met young people and their families, as we filmed all over the world, for a short time I became part of a different culture. Their food was different, the sing-song of their language was different, their clothes and skin colours were often different. Their creative forms were different. Different than what I had experienced growing up here in Canada. And in each case I was excited and enriched by experiencing and sharing all these differences.

Not just enriched. But changed. My own horizons grew and therefore my own consciousness expanded. The best way I've heard this expressed, in my life, was by a fine spiritual teacher who said "consciousness loves contrast." I have found this to be true again and again: whether it's making that television series, or learning to skydive through the air, or scuba dive in the oceans or venture into different cultural experiences here in Toronto, like being here this evening with all of you. Every time I break the mold of my habit patterns I find life more and more enriching.

Perhaps because I was born here, I find Canadian culture a little boring, which is why I love traveling. And, of course, we're a very young culture. So when you bring your Korean culture here to Canada, you are actually bringing the gift of yourselves to us.

In Canada, we often miss the rich and wonderful multicultural creativity that is thriving all around us, like the Korean poetry that Dae-Tong is writing in his and Maria's corner variety store, where I buy lottery tickets and occasionally a Pepsi. And that brings me back to this evening. It is an honour, that enriches my life, to be here with you and to be included in the first publication of the Korean-Canadian Literary Forum-21.

I thank you all for sharing yourselves with me.

*Also published in Variety Crossing 2.*

# 서로 다른것을 선호하는 의식: 복합문화의 창의성

폴 살츠만
영화제작가, 선라이즈영화사 사장

신사숙녀 여러분 안녕하세요.
여러분과 이 자리를 함께하게 된 것을 영광으로 생각하며 기쁩니다. 백지문학회에서 펴내는 Forum-21 창간호에 저의 단시 2편이 실리게 되어 영광스럽고 이는 저의 처녀작품이 활자화 된 것이어서 기쁘지 않을 수가 없습니다. 이는 또한
저의 세상 바라보는 정서가 넓어졌다는데 더욱 기쁘지 않을 수가 없습니다. 여러분과 함께 이 축제의 기쁨을 나누고 아울러 허대통씨 내외분과 남선생님 그리고 최선생님을 만나 뵙게 됨으로서 저의 삶은 훨씬 풍요로와 졌으며, 이에관하여 몇 말씀 드리고자 합니다.

저의 직업은 영화를 만드는 일입니다. 1965년 부터 TV와 영화의 일에 몸을 담은 이래, 저는 240편의 드라마와 약 60편의 기록 영화를 제작 했습니다. 지난 35년 넘게 이러한 일을 하는 과정에서 로보트 레드포을 만나고, 오드리 헵펀과 포옹도 했으며 두 차례의 에미상과 그밖에 여러 영화상을 받는 등 많은 즐거움이 있었습니만, 영화을 많드는 사람으로서 제가 누릴수 있었던 가장 큰 기쁨은 26편의 연속 기록영화를 만드는 일 이었습니다.

22개국을 필름에 담은 것인데, 각기 다른 문화권에서 젊은 이들의 창의력과 한 세대에서 다음세대로 전수되어 온 창조적 전통의 모습에 초점을 맞춘 것이지요. 각 편을 제작하는 과정에서 그들의 가족들을 만나면서 전 세계를 필름에 담은 것인데, 그러는 동안 저는 잠시나마 각기 다른 문화를 접촉하게 된 것입니다. 음식이 다르고, 부르는 노래와 말이 다르고, 의복과 피부색도 달랐습니다.

이들의 창작 형식도 이 곳 캐나다에서 성장 하면서 경험한 것과는 달랐습니다.
그리고 그때마다 서로 다른 경험을 함께 나누면서, 저는 많은 감동을 받았으며, 더할나이 없이 풍요로 왔습니다. 단순한 풍요로움이 아니라 하나의 변화였습니다.

저 자신의 삶에 지평이 넓어 졌으며, 따라서 제 개인의 의식의 폭도 넓어진 것입니다. 저의 생애에서 들은 가장 좋은 표현의 방법으로 정신적 훌륭한 스승의 말씀 [서로 다른 것을 선호하는 의식] 이라는 것입니다. 이말이 진실임을 저는 보면서 거듭 거듭 체험 했습니다.

TV 시리즈를 제작할 때, 공중에서 스카이 다이빙을 배울 때도, 바다에서 스쿠버 다이빙을 배울 때나 이곳 토론토에서 오늘 저녁 여러분과 함께 하면서 서로 다른 문화의 경험을 하면서 그 속에 담긴 아름다운 진실을 보아 왔습니다. 그 때마다 저의 습관 이패턴의 틀을 깨며 저 자신의 삶이 도욱 풍요로움을 발견합니다.

어쩌면 저는 여기서 태어났기 때문에 캐나의 문화에 다소 싫증을 느꼈는지 몰라도, 그래서 그런지 저는 여행을 좋아합니다. 물론 캐나다 문화는 성장하고 있습니다.

이런때에 여러분은 캐나다에 한국고유문화를 가져왔으며, 사실은 여러분 자신을 캐나다인들에게 선물로 주는 셈입니다. 캐나다에서 사는 우리는 곳곳에 산재한 풍부하고 훌륭한 복합문화을 위하여 창작의 중요성을 지나칠 때가 많습니다.

허대통씨가 그의 가게에서 쓰고 있는 한국말 시도 그런 경우지요. 저는 그의 가게에서 복권도 사고 더러는 팹시도 사 마십니다만, 그런 인연으로 오늘저녁 이 자리에 오게 되었습니다. 이렇게 여러분과 자리을 함께 하고 한카문학 Forum-21의 창간호에 참여하게 된 것은 저의 영광이며, 저의 삶을 살지게 합니다.
여러분의 친교에 감사드립니다.

*Translated by Dae-Tong Huh. Also published in Variety Crossing 2.*

# The Heart's Garden

Kyung-Whan Yoo

From time to time I ask myself, at what age did I start remembering things? The answer is always four. So it is as if my childhood started when I was four years old. The bedroom where I listened to my mother reading a book, the image of the warm copper stove reflected in the closet mirror that was called "Euguri" are some memories I can pick out.

The societal change that occurred in the 1930s has been firmly imprinted on my mind. The more my mind was filled with whatever I saw and whatever I heard with no space to spare, I longed for open space. This space extended to a world beyond sight. It seems like that was the motivation behind why I still like roaming around wide open places.

After retirement, my stage was downsized. I only visited the galleries in Insadong, and looking at the mountains and rivers in the artwork became a habit, like the inertia of office work before retirement. The fun world laughs at me as if it is a Chang, Uk Jin picture, but I greatly enjoyed the afternoons I spent searching the alleys of this world.

Although it seems awkward, genuine life is revealed only through a pattern stained with laughter and tears. Perhaps my age is to blame for the failing eyes that were able to look upon life optimistically but the pattern of life only makes me dizzy now.

Even with age, there are some things you must remember. It is the fact that the leaves of compassion sprout on my "Abandoned Self," and grow even faster than bean sprouts to fill my heart. "Loneliness" does not grow mold even if left alone, but "Yearning" constantly throws tantrums, filling the heart like the bean sprout jar. Not being able to come across anything in the day-today life that can touch the heart, so yearning grows and grows.

These days, it is not the mountains but the fields that make my heart green. When I stand on the edge of a completely open field, the joy that comes from looking into the future greets me like the wind. Then, the burden of life that I was barely able to drag along during the winter, disappears without any trace and I feel the lightness; it feels like sitting on feathers that were shed.

The field with countless wildflowers, their names unknown to me, are spread out. This place approaches me as if it had been waiting for me. It is like a carpet woven by God's hand so I get excited looking at the sparkling gems. You cannot take these gems with you after death; instead I take walks and collect them, putting them away in my heart while I am alive. Such walks are my leisure and are incomparable with anything else.

Instead of walking the city blocks, now I walk the outskirts of life's arena. Everywhere my line of vision can reach, I consider my garden. If greater happiness exists, it must be a hallucination. As the color of the "We Love Green" group ripens in our society, I call my inner child and prod him to take another look at the world. Then I ask what I see now. My inner child responds quietly that he sees the color of my hometown garden just before spring.

One young print maker (no longer young now) said that when you live in Jechun Bakdaljae like a farmer, all the mountains and rivers are sacred books. The reason that I still remember this statement is that I was envious ever since I heard him say this. I was unable to go into Jechun Bakdaljae but I searched many alleys instead.

I used to sit on the end chair or low chair so that I would not have to socialize with office superiors. I thought that I had to do that in order for my stories to be amusing. The end or the lower seats are where you first see and smell the people walking powerfully like the windy alleys. This is how affection grows.

After my childhood, my dreams during my adolescence formed a triangle. Puppy love, allowance, and an ego to walk with my chin held high. However, the moment I threw away the school cap of my adolescence, this triangle started to become distorted. But even so, the memories of those times that fill my heart are as precious as gold. There is no better comfort to me than these valuable memories nowadays.

Attitude is very important in the relationship of the body and mind in health. It is reported that the occurrence of cancer is apparently low in developmentally challenged people. This is the contemporary interpretation of the words of an old monk who said that the heart is the master.

One soldier, a survivor of the trench, said that the dead are happier than the living. This confession of hatred for war comes from his experience. However, we lead easy lives but our hatred explodes on inappropriate matters which shocks others and hurts ourselves.

Like a verse from an old poem, "I've looked the whole day for spring and did not meet it, but when I looked to the branch of a Japanese apricot tree, there it was," I cannot hide my happiness when I meet the wildflowers dancing in the wind of the wide field in the outskirts of my life arena.

No matter how much you travel, beautiful scenery is in the heart. Even if you see impressive scenery and marvel at it, the feeling is only momentary because you cannot stay for long. The lingering memory is the footprint that is left on the heart. This is the garden of my heart.

It is not only the river that quietly flows, but also does the heart that watches something flowing. It is the same with the yearning for green. The field's color that was absorbed by my childhood eyes as happiness, without anyone knowing, is pushing up green little by little inside of me.

*English translation by Hyeamin Yoon. Also published in Variety Crossing 9.*

# April and Literature

By Kijo Song

Spring has long ago pushed open the door and entered the room. April tempts me with its warm sun to step outside, but instead, I direct my gaze towards Namsan Mountain. Namsan Mountain hides behind the thin fog-like layer hanging between the high-rise buildings. Whether the layer is due to yellow sand or air pollution is uncertain but it mirrors the stifling feeling in my chest.

The cold and depressing winter has returned home and it has been a long time since April has come. As I bathe in spring's lethargy, I think back on the past 50 years of writing – never once have I tired of "doing literature." I would have complained of the pains and have quit any other work nearly as tiring but why do I still enjoy writing even to this day?

I cannot rid myself of the affection I feel for people and as long as I am a human, I cannot ignore the problems of human beings. Poet Chi-Hwan Yu said that there is no meaningful literature without such interest and affection nor would there be literature that truly fulfills human beings' needs. I agree. After countless changings of seasons, and as I enter my old age past my lively youth, I continue to write because of my love for people and my love for life. Literature is the very record of people and life.

To lead a refined lifestyle, one must step into the world of literature and live immersed in it. Therefore, literature is not the possession of a few but a public heritage of which everyone has joint ownership. However, people say that literature has degraded. If literature is life's record and its mirror, one can conclude that life has degraded just as much. After all, literature is an imitation of life. It does not clone life as it is though; its purpose lies in describing the good and beautiful and turning the pains of life into joy. So, literature is gentle, warm, good, and beautiful. It does not leave a person scarred. Just as the freezing dizzle of spring rain bores a hole and makes a flower blossom, literature approaches us, opens our hearts, and helps us realize our wrongs. In addition, it gives us wisdom to look into the days to come and have faith in our ambitions and hopes.

Just 50 years ago, youths were scolded and warned of the harm that reading novels or memorizing poems could do. Only textbooks were acceptable. Ironically, today's Korean language textbooks are filled almost entirely with such literature. Literature that was once avoided for fear of leading a youth down the wrong path is being used as a teaching tool. The reason is none other than the fact that literature is the genuine record of life.

Electronic media have swept the world and the computer/internet culture has an unyielding hold, but as long as paper exists, literature will continue to evolve and books will continue to be made. In reality, literature provides the framework and the contents of all electronic media products. Even based on this consideration alone, one can place literature on the topmost seat of art and humanity.

It is sad that one does not consider literature as a core art but tends to neglect it. One worries that "when literature dies and life ends/ when even the truth of love abandons the shadow of love and hatred," the world will be over. This is a passage from In-whan Pak's poem, The Wooden Horse and the Lady. If literature, love, and truth did not exist, what would become of this world? I ponder with the hope that literature will blossom like the flowers of April.

*English translation by Hyeamin Yoon. Also published in Variety Crossing 8.*

# Wor-a Spring

HAE MYUNG BYUN

The sky is like blue glass. We go, through daylight unimpeded by even the slightest trace of wind, to Myeongsa Mountain (鳴沙山)[1]. The first character, myeong (明), refers to the cry of a bird, the second, sa (沙) means sand; it received its name because when the wind brushes against the sand it sounds much like the chattering of birds. The mountain is found in a desert in Dunhwang (敦煌). The blaze of the sun will overwhelm you, though you cover your face with a towel tucked under your hat and wear coloured glasses.

A golden sand-dune. A field of golden sand. A cosmos of golden sand. The surf of sand-waves beats a mountain ridge rising up from the plain like a knife. I ride a camel from the base of Myeongsa Mountain and just as if I were in the caravan of a great merchant, slowly, ever so slowly, in the pace of days gone by, I go up towards the mountain. The camel's pace, as it trots over the sand, is slow and lethargic.

As we descend deeply into the shade of Myeongsa Mountain I am stupefied to see in this plain of sand, in this cosmos of nothing but sand, a pavilion, rising up from the desert like a mirage. There I can see a forest – a small forest with a few trees.

While my party, unbothered by the heat, continues to travel up Myeongsa Mountain I walk on my own to Wor-a Spring (月牙泉)[2].

They say that the wind blowing up the mountain ridge originates from Wor-a Spring. Therefore it is said that in Wor-a Spring there are no sandstorms.

A few people who look like Chinese tourists are sitting in the pavilion drinking tea. I pass a small garden and see a few old willow trees and

1 *Chinese Mingsha*
2 *Chinese Yueya*

elms. Beneath the trees is a little lake like a half moon. From the lake one hears the babbling of blue water. This is not water – this is emotion, this is wonder, this is felicity. Though the sandstorm blows violently about us, not a speck of sand has entered the water. Even the hot desert sun does not dare to evaporate this lake. For several thousand years it has been in the same spot. Even now, an unceasing spring fills this lake that looks like the back teeth of the moon, like a half-moon. That is why it is called Wor-a Spring – Wor (月) refers to the moon, A (牙) refers to back teeth.
As I stand in front of this mysterious lake in the desert, I find myself unable to repress my happiness – I want to shout out and let people know. I watch the people walking along the ridge of Myeongsa Mountain. Those people moving along the ridge of Myeongsa Mountain look like little dots. They say new sand rises up to replace sand the slips down from the ridge. Myeongsa Mountain's height remains the same.
Snow accumulating for 10,000 years on the Tianshan Mountains melts and flows under the ground. This water becomes the Wor-a Spring – when it rises to the ground, it creates this oasis.

I hide Wor-a Spring deep in my heart
Waiting for you!
The night birds singing under the sickle moon
Wake Myeongsa Mountain from its slumber.

Myeongsa Mountain is beautiful because of Wor-a Spring. The desert is not frightening because of Wor-a Spring. Hope is not lost because once a long time ago we realized that beneath the land flows a river.
Our lives are truly beautiful. In the depths of our hearts we hide love as big as a sickle moon. In the most parched periods of our lives we hide a treasure. I saw this when I walked up Myeongsa Mountain.

*English Translation by Adam Bohnet. Also published in Variety Crossing 5.*

## Korean Literary Forum-21 Celebrates Asian Heritage

By Ben Viccari

CEMA President Ben Viccari's Address at the Asian Heritage Month celebrations organized at the University of Toronto's Hart House by the Korean-Canadian Literary Forum-21.

I'm ambling through Little Italy and pause at the Balfour bookstore on College St where I look through the one-dollar bin outside. Serendipity takes over. Here's Cyril Connolly's anthology from his literary magazine Horizon published between 1939 and 1944 and here's a poem I've been trying to find a very long time.

It's by Alun Lewis, the young Welsh soldier-poet who died in an accident in Burma in 1944 and it was written three years earlier while he was still in England. It begins:

All day it has rained, and we on the edge of the moors
Have sprawled in our bell tents, moody and dull as boors

Now I have the entire poem. All I've remembered are those two lines; for me they summed up the soul deadening sense of boredom that exists for soldiers in waiting but from which I was rescued by reading novels, essays and verses that challenged and stretched my imagination. I progressed from the humdrum to poetry by Keats, Shelley, Eliot and Thomas and criticism by the likes of Virginia Woolf and Raymond Mortimer.

Apart from this liberation from boredom, this reading helped me realize we were fighting a war for the kind of freedom that good writing and poetry, in particular, stands for.

And that is why I am here to bring to Dae-Tong Huh [President of Literary Forum-21 and all of you the good wishes of the Canadian Ethnic Media Association for the success of this event.

The Association began 28 years ago when Sierhey Khmara Ziniak, the outspoken editor/publisher of the Byelorussian Voice took exception to the existing ethnic media association an organization that accepted as members publishers of print media only. No room for editors, columnists, reporters or broadcasters. No room for independent writers. In addition, Sierhey Ziniak was a poet as well as a newspaperman.

As an all-inclusive association we are proud that CEMA includes a number of poets, among whom is Romanian-born Flavia Cosma who just 10 days ago was here at Hart House for the launching of her latest book Leaves of a Diary. The foreword to the book was written by Dr. George Elliott Clarke, another member: and there are more: Mara Serbin, Masood Khan and others

And so Dae-Tong, we salute you for the honour you do to international poets in the true spirit of multiculturalism and in closing offer these words that you wrote in our anthology of members works, Mosaic in Media:

You are man and woman, nothing else
You are young and old, nothing else
You are good and bad, nothing else.
Learn to love for love should be a part of you
Remember my friend
Listen to your heart
Before money and power

*Also published in Variety Crossing 8.*

# Short Story

# Mermaid

Barry Callaghan

He woke up hearing the ocean. He closed his eyes as if he were still asleep and listened because he was nowhere near an ocean. He had been born in a concentration camp and he had survived the camp and made a life for himself selling insurance and now he was sixty-years old and having never been to an ocean he was in bed with a woman who thought she was old because she was thirty-eight and he thought she was young because she was thirty-eight. It was her bed; the pillows were of soft down.

"Do you hear the ocean?" he asked. He had never slept all night in anyone else's bed.

She opened an eye. Her left eye. It was a pale ice blue, it was a blue clock, he thought.

He couldn't remember her having blue eyes.

"Yes," she said. "I love swimming in the ocean."

"You do?"

"Yes."

He was worried that if she opened her other eye it would be blue, too.

"I was sure you had brown eyes," he said.

"Because I'm a mermaid," she said. "All mermaids have brown eyes."

She laughed. Her teeth were very white and the tip of her tongue between her teeth was pink. She drew his head down to her belly, between her thighs. He took a deep breath.

He could smell the ocean.

He tasted the ocean.

"Only great men have ever slept with a mermaid," she said and opened her other eye.

It was blue.

"You're no mermaid," he said.

"Welcome to the real world," she said.

"No, no," he said.

He was still strong, lean and muscular. He made a fist and showed her the inside of his forearm, a tattoo.

It was a mermaid.

"You've got a mermaid tattoo on your arm," she said.

"No, look very hard, he said, and he drew her head down to his arm.

She said his skin smelled like smoke, she had smelled it all night. He said, "No, just look, look hard."

She looked and at last she said, "Numbers. There's numbers inside the mermaid."

He said, "Yes, they disappeared in my little mermaid."

"Why'd you do that?" she asked as she lay back in her soft bed.

She looked almost unbearably young to him.

"Because I am alive and she is now my real world. She has brown eyes and those others who gave me the numbers are dead and they had blue eyes," and he leaned over her and lightly kissed her eyes closed and said, "Now we make love again."

# 인어

## 배리 칼라한

그는 잠에서 깨어나 바다 소리를 듣는다. 그는 아직도 잠에 취한 듯이 눈을 감은채 주위에서는 볼수 없는 바다 소리를 잠결에서 듣게 된다. 그는 강제 수용소에서 태어났고 그는 야영지에서 살아 남아 그 와중에 그는 보험을 팔아 생계를 유지해 왔다. 지금은 어느 덧 육십살이 되었지만 바다에는 가 본적이 없었다. 마음에 드는 여인과 침실을 같이하고 있었는데 그녀는 나이 38세로, 자신은 나이가 많다고 생각했고 반면에 남자는 그녀 나이 38세로는 용모가 젊어 보인다고 생각했다. 그녀는 안락한 침대에 베개을 베고 누워 있었다.

여보 저 바다 소리가 들리오? 그는 나직히 묻는다. 그는 남의 침대에서 밤을 새어 본 적이 없다.

그녀가 한쪽 눈을 떴다. 왼쪽 눈은 창백한 담청색에 푸른 시계 모형이라고 그는 생각 했다.

그녀가 푸른눈을 가지고 있었는지 그는 기억할 수 없다.

왜 놀라세요, 그녀는 반문 하듯이,

"나는요 바다수영을 무척좋아 하거든요"

그래?

"아주요"

그는 그녀가 다른 눈을 뜨면 그 눈도 푸른 눈일까 걱정이 되어서다.

"당신의 눈은 갈색 이라고 생각했었는데, 하며 말을 건냈다.

"나는요, 인어이니까," 그녀는 대꾸했다. "모는 인어들은 갈색 눈을 하고있지요"

그녀는 폭소한다. 그녀의 치아는 아주 흰색에 혀 끝은 분홍색을 띠우고 이었다. 그녀의 허벅지 사이로 자신의 머리를 복부까지 꾸부렸다. 그는 심호흡을 했다.

그는 그녀로부터 바다 냄새를 맡는다.

그는 바다를 맛 본것이다.

"저명한 인사들 만이 인어와 잠자리를 같이 하지요", 말하고 나서 그녀의 다른 눈을 열었다.

푸른눈 이였다.

"당신은 인어가 아니잖아," 그는 말했다.

"현실 세계에 오심을 환영합니다," 그녀는 말했다.

아니, 이런일이, 그는 기가 막힌듯 말했다.

그는 아직도 강인하고, 지방이 없는 근육 체질이다. 그는 주먹을 쥐고는 그의 팔뚝에 세겨진 문신을 그녀에게 보였다.

그 문신은 인어의 표시였다.

"당신팔에는 인어의 문신이 새겨져 있네요," 그녀는 놀난 듯이 말했다.

아니, 자세히 보라고, 그는 말했다, 그리고는 그는 그녀의 머리를 그의 팔로 끌어 앉았다.

그녀는 그의 살갓에서 풍겨 나오는 연기같은 냄새가 좋아, 그녀는 밤새 그 냄새을 맡았다. 그는 말 하길, 아니, 건성으로 보지 말고, 더 세심히 드려다 보라니까."

살펴 보고는, 마침내 그녀는 놀라면서, "숫자" 그것은 인어들만의 비밀의 숫자.

그는 말했다, 왜 그리 놀래, "이것은 내 어린인어 시절의 흔적이야."

어떻게 된거에요? 그녀는 보드라운 잠자리에 누은채 반문 했다.

그녀는 믿기 어려울 만치 그에게 아주 어리게 보였다.

"내가 살아 있기에 그녀가 나의 현실에 살고 있다. 그녀는 갈색눈이었느데 세상을 떠난 그들이 그녀에게 준 숫자는 푸른눈 이었다," 그는 그녀에게 기대어 눈을 감고 있는 그녀에게 부드러운 키스을 하며, 속삭이는 말로, " 오늘도 우리는 사랑하고 있잖아."

# In The Right Place

DAVID MACFARLANE

It could be successfully argued – if, like me, you're sitting alone in a room and there's no one around to argue back – that at the most basic level of definition an artist is someone who gets the right thing in the right place. This is not as simple as it sounds. If you believe that right things have a natural inclination toward right places, then I can safely say that you have never met the electrician who first worked on our house. Or, if you have, you were smart enough not to leave him alone to decide where a few light switches, and plugs, and phone jacks should go.

For instance: there were an infinite number of possible wrong notes and possible wrong places for notes on the scores that Handel faced when, in August and September of 1741, he composed The Messiah. But somehow – and the thought crossed my mind just the other day while I was trying to move a piano in order to plug in the lights of a Christmas tree – Handel missed them all. He either so brilliantly avoided mistakes he got everything right, or so brilliantly got everything right, he avoided mistakes. But whatever he did, he did not put the phone jack behind the door to the dining room.

Or, in his 1927 poem, The Journey of the Magi, T.S. Eliot might have chosen any number of words for the fourth and fifth line. But he wrote this: "The ways deep and the weather sharp, The very dead of winter." And, somehow that straightforward description of the hardships faced by the three kings on their improbable journey, coming at that very spot in the poem, not only got the thing right, it got the business of getting the right thing in the right place right, too.

In the same way, there could be no one more right than Mr. Prothero in Dylan Thomas's A Child's Christmas in Wales. And on the afternoon of Christmas Eve, while Mrs. Prothero is shouting "Fire!" Mr. Prothero could be nowhere in the universe more right than in his living-room, smacking at the smoke with a slipper and saying, "A fine Christmas!"

Getting the right word, or image, or idea in the absolute right place is essentially what poetry is – or so you can convincingly argue in the solitary confinement that is a writer's basement office. What poetry isn't, is the wall in our upstairs hall where we might have hung a picture were it not for the fact that all of the wall's square footage is dedicated to having a light switch in the middle of it.

If you have set aside some time to watch the 1951 film version of A Christmas Carol this year (and if you have not, I encourage you to revisit your holiday schedule), you can watch the transformed Ebenezer Scrooge struggle to keep a straight face after he pretends to bark "Cratchit! You're late." And you can think: of all the gestures and expressions and intonations and movement that Alastair Sim could have used in that scene, how did he know what to do and when to do it so that his performance would attain the giddy, joyous perfection that it does? The toss of the quill pen over his shoulder is, in the dramatic conjoining of thing and place, about as right as right can get. It's a perfection that is difficult to analyze, I admit. But its non-intuitive, un-creative, anti-improvisational, and stubbornly obtuse opposite is something I may well have encountered when I came home to find the electrician carving a hole in a wooden Victorian door-frame in order to accommodate his chosen position for a plug.

The right-thing-in-the-right-place theory of artistic creation is a good rule-of-thumb to use in figuring out what to think of the latest creation of the British artist, Martin Creed (a room in which the lights go on and off) and of a recent installation at the Banff School (if you don't already know what it is, you might prefer to keep it that way). These displays of the avant-garde have managed, as these controversies always do, to capture the attention of people who spend most of their time paying art no attention at all. The Banff School, for instance, devotes itself to supporting the hard work and in many cases, the genius, of an astonishing array of artists. But we don't hear very much about them. That's because there's nothing about art that so captivates people who aren't interested in art as a heated debate about what art isn't. I guess they'd know.

Whether Work #27, the lights going on and off, is art, or is merely the job our electrician took after he finished here, is hard to say. When it comes to putting the right thing in the right place, you never know. That's the thing about great art: it's surprising. And that's the thing about not-great art: it isn't. To begin with, there's the question of finding the right thing in the first place. Notice that the phrase does not leave many loopholes lying around for Sunday painters, hobbyists, and "creative types" to squirm through. It doesn't say "getting one of the right things," or "one of the right-ish things." It says: "the right thing..." And choosing the one right thing out of so very many possible wrong ones is a risky business. It's a miraculous undertaking, really – the artistic equivalent of seeing a star in the east in the very dead of winter and deciding that you're going to see where it might take you.

Unfortunately, there are lots of people who don't believe that the risk of failure, or the uncertainty of inspiration, or the danger of the unknown are worth all the trouble. Most of our cities bear their stamp wherever we look. These people don't have anything against beauty, exactly; they are just distrustful of the mysterious process that produces it. The way they see it, if a plug works, it doesn't matter where it is. If a switch turns on a light, it hardly matters that it gets in the way of a painting. The right thing in the right place is not, for them, a miracle to be sought. If, for some reason, a star had led them to the east, they would have stopped at the inn for a nice dinner, and would never have gone out back to see what was happening in the barn.

*Also published in Variety Crossing 4.*

# I Love Canada

Harry J. Huang (Freeman J. Wong)

The citizenship judge asked for Joel's name, address and occupation. Joel did well with his name, but got into trouble with the words "address" and "occupation."

"What do you do?" the judge asked, trying to make it easier for him. "How do you make a living?" Joel was still blinking at the judge. "Teacher? Factory worker? Driver? Cook?"

"Me. Cook."

"How many children do you have? Children? Kids? Babies?"

"Five."

"You are wonderful. You know so little English, but you are able to support your family."

Joel thought the judge was asking him another question, so he answered quickly, "I love Canada." The judge was very pleased.

"How many provinces are there in Canada?" the judge smiled.

"I love Canada."

"What are the rights and duties of a Canadian citizen?"

"I love Canada."

The judge had been told that his colleague was sick and he had to help preside over the citizenship ceremony on his behalf. "Now let me ask you one more question," said the judge. "Do you like Canada?"

"I love Canada."

"There you go. You have passed the citizenship examination." The judge signed a form and handed it over to Joel, shaking hands with him as he showed him out of the office.

Joel was very worried. He didn't know what the judge meant. Near the elevator, he showed his form to another applicant who spoke his mother tongue, "What's this?"

"It's a notice informing you that you have passed the citizenship examination and you are going to attend the ceremony on Monday."

"What does it mean?"

"It means you are going to sing the national anthem and become a Canadian citizen."

"Oh, Canada," Joel sang to the tune of the Canadian national anthem. Then he shouted, "I love Canada."

*Also published in Variety Crossing 7.*

# 我爱加拿大（小小说）

黄俊雄 (Harry J. Huang)（加拿大）

公民法官满口英语问乔尔叫什么名字、住在哪儿、职业是什么。乔尔的名字答对了，但听不懂“address”（地址）和“occupation”（职业）的意思。于是，法官用更简单的词语问他。

“你是干什么的？怎么谋生的?”

乔尔对着法官直眨眼。

法官接着问：“是老师？工人？司机？厨师?”

“我，厨师。”

“你有几个孩子？小孩？儿童？婴儿？”

“五个。”

“你真了不起。你的英语水平这么低，竟能养活一家子。”

乔尔以为法官又在问他一个什么问题，便赶快回答说：“我爱加拿大。”

法官很满意，接着笑咪咪问乔尔：“加拿大有多少个省？”

“我爱加拿大。”

“加拿大公民的权利和义务是什么？”

“我爱加拿大。”

此时，法官接通知他的同事生病，要他去代替主持一个公民入籍宣誓仪式。

“这样吧，”法官说，“我再问你最后一个问题。你喜欢不喜欢加拿大？”

“我爱加拿大。”　　　　“好的！你的公民考试通过了。”法官签了个表格，交给乔尔，一边同他握手一边把他送出办公室。乔尔忧心忡忡，不知道法官说了些什么。走到电梯旁边，他把表格拿给会讲自己母语的另一位入籍申请者看。“这是什么？”

“是通知你，你已经通过公民考试，下星期一参加入籍宣誓仪式。”

“这是什么意思？”

“你就要唱国歌，当加拿大公民啦！”

“啊，加拿大！”乔尔哼起了加拿大国歌的调子。接着，蓦然大喊一声“我爱加拿大。”

[注]“Oh, Canada”是加拿大国歌的头两个词。

# Moon Child

HELEN KANG

The night is heavy with expectations. The weather forecast claimed overnight rain, but the moon shines dubiously. Half full, it glows with an organic radiance. Standing in the backyard of mom's house and looking up at the moon, I am reminded of the time when I got lost in the woods.

Mom and I had gone on a camping trip and I must have strayed from the group somehow during a hike. It was dark and eerie, and I was on the verge of tears when I discovered the moon hanging in the sky, except to me it wasn't a moon. It looked to me like Mom's fatty eyelids. She was reclining, her head tilted to one side. Her night-black hair fell over her brows, exposing only one glowing eyelid. I curled up on the grass, comforted by her milky gaze, and fell asleep. I was woken up by Mom hugging me and crying frantically. I cupped her cheeks in my hands and laughed in delight. The half moon had descended from the sky and became two puffy eyes on her face.

It was one of the rare moments that I saw Mom cry. Even when she caught her hand in an old industrial sewing machine at the factory and severed the tip of her left pinky, she didn't shed a tear or let out a yelp. So the aunties at the factory told me. I can recall only one other occasion where I caught her weeping. I'd woken up in the night at the sound of someone crying, and I found Mom sitting by her wooden dresser box. She was holding a small piece of white paper to her bosom, head hung and shoulders jerking from time to time. I meant to ask her what was wrong and stroke her hair, but sleep paralyzed me. As I drifted off to sleep, Mom lifted her head to reveal her swollen eyes, even fatter than usual. Then, I dreamt of a princess trapped on a boat in the middle of a lake with no oars. She cried and cried, and a giant hippopotamus drank her tears. It drank and drank until it got so fat that even its eyelids were fat, like Mom's eyes.

Single-slit, and fat with swallowed tears.

"What are you doing outside, Jung-ah?" Aunt Maria breaks my trance as she peers out of the screen door. "You'll be feasted on by mosquitoes. Hurry inside."

"In a minute, Eemo."

She intends to say something more, but shakes her head and returns to the darkness of the kitchen. Eemo and I have come to a truce since Mom's death. We used to dash at each other's throats whenever we had the chance, driving Mom crazy. Her two closest kin are each other's worst enemy, Mom used to say. She would play the go-between, skillfully placating both of us with sweet words allegedly from the other party of the dispute. Eemo is six years younger than Mom, and we were more like siblings than aunt and niece when it came to attracting Mom's attention. We silently agreed that our petty fights were merely a means of getting Mom to pamper us.

I guess with Mom gone, neither of us finds the game enjoyable. There's no purpose to our disagreements. And with my imminent trip, our mutual silence has deepened further into awkwardness.

Up to a few weeks after Mom's funeral, she was still attacking me. I remember asking her where Mom's sewing kit was, holding a button and a sweater in my hand rather helplessly, but she didn't look up from the dishes. I suppose she found it disgraceful that the daughter of a seamstress didn't know where her Mom's sewing things were, let alone know how to work her Singer.

"Check the dresser beside her bed..." She went on, but I couldn't understand the rest because she spoke quickly in difficult Korean. She did it on purpose, I knew, because I was used to Mom speaking to me in simple Korean. Eemo used to tell Mom that she treated me like a twenty-five-year-old child. At that moment, I felt resentful in knowing that there was truth in what she said.

Thus, I had to go into Mom's room by myself, which I didn't like to do since her funeral. It wasn't that I was especially superstitious, but I didn't feel that I had the authority to be there. As though afraid to be discovered, I tiptoed around the room and knelt beside her dresser box. The little wooden antique dresser was Mom's treasure. Mom said it used to belong to her mother. It is built in the old Korean style with a lock that fits a little golden key, which Mom used to keep in her pocket. The faded key in my hand, I unlocked the drawers, and as I did, I caught a glimpse of myself in the mirror that was propped on top. They say that daughters resemble their mothers as they age. It seems like I'm an exception. "You look just like your mother" wasn't one of the comments I received often, even as a child. Searching through the dresser, I realized that the last time I did this was when I was ten years old. The rummaging had to stop then because Mom discovered me and began locking it. The contents were different, but the feeling was familiar: probing into Mom's things, invading her privacy, invading her past. I inhaled the musty smell of time in the aged wood.

At last I found the sewing kit, but something else caught my eye. It was a very old photo. What puzzled me were not its dog-eared edges or the yellowish hue, but the person in it. It was a photo of a man with deep creases over the eyelids.

"Jung-Ah, what are you doing?"

Mom never called me by my English name, Julie. Even when I had my Canadian friends over, she called me by my Korean name. It used to embarrass me when I was a teenager, when being babied by your parents is totally uncool. When I dyed my hair red-brown and pierced my belly-button, to Mom I was still Jung-Ah, the little girl in jet-black pig-tails.

"Jung-Ah, stop it! Look, your eyes are red."

I was sitting in front of the mirror of her dresser and briskly rubbing my eyes. I was seven years old. When Mom finally tore my hands away, my eyes were swollen and red.

"What do you think you're doing?"

"Umma, why do I have these lines?"

"What lines?"

I pointed to my double-slit eyelids. I outlined the creases in the thin skin, the marks of beauty for which many Korean females turn to plastic surgery. Mom sighed then smiled.

"They're called ssang-guh-pool. See, they make your eyes look big and pretty."

She sat me in front of the mirror again. There we were, sitting side by side, mother and daughter. And yet it was difficult to make that out. My eyes were swollen but the creases were still visible. Mom's single-slit eyes still looked puffier than mine. I burst into tears. I was too young to articulate myself. How was I able to explain to her that the lines over my eyes were like two giant canyons separating me from her?

A week after discovering the photo, I received a letter addressed to my Korean name.

"Eemo, can you read this and translate it for me?"

Eemo took the envelope and pored over it curiously. Then, her expression changed as though she bit into a chunk of ginger, and she shoved the envelope into her pocket.

"Oh, it's nothing. Don't worry about it."

I snatched the letter from her. It was typical of my aunt to treat me like a child. I was about to protest, but her expression was so peculiar that I stopped myself.

"Do what you like, Jung-Ah. You're a grown woman after all."

The next day, I purchased a Korean-English dictionary and began translating the letter. It was only a page long, but it took long hours of searching for every word in the dictionary. I knew it was from a man from Mom's hometown back in Korea, but the rest didn't come so easily. I didn't ask Eemo for help. I was determined to decipher it myself. It was a new game for me, like a jigsaw puzzle, except that I didn't have a finished picture to work with. The puzzle was beginning to look like Mom's mouth. It was laughing, but I couldn't hear the laughter.

"Why do I have these lines on my eyes, umma? You don't have it."
Mom removed the icepack from my reddened eyes.

"It's because appa had them. It's because you look just like him."

"Daddy? I have a daddy?"
Mom never talked about my father much. She told me a very brief and vague story about how father was in the Korean navy and died at sea.

"And so I brought you here, to Canada, where little children don't get pointed at for not having a daddy."
Then she hugged me and I couldn't see her face. I thought it strange that anyone would point at children in the first place. But I liked the sound of my father dying heroically in the navy. I had dreams about him saving Mom while she was drowning in the sea.

There was one incident that made me wonder if Mom herself really believed in what she told me. It was at a luncheon at my Saturday Korean school. The children had prepared small snacks for the parents and the families were gathered around a huge table eating sushi and rice cakes. The parents began talking. Actually, the dads talked and the moms listened. The men were very loud and they seemed to have a lot to say. Oddly enough, Mom said nothing. Not a single word. This was a woman whose voice can carry over the loud conversations of ten women at her monthly potlucks. And now, she was silent. She was smiling and nodding. I found discomfort in her silence and tugged at her hand.

"Shh! Jung-Ah, be quiet."

I wanted to tell her not to worry. I wanted to remind her that no one in Canada points at people for not having a daddy. But she seemed to have forgotten what she had told me. It was as though she was the little girl without a father, shrinking at invisible fingers that pointed at her.

While I translated the letter, Eemo kept her distance from me. I knew from the tension that I was doing something forbidden, perhaps damaging. But I couldn't stop. With every word of the letter translated, every phrase deciphered, every paragraph understood, I was unveiling Mom. It was like searching through her dresser box.

"Do you remember what umma said the morning she died, Eemo?"

"Huh? What do you mean?"

"She told me to go to her hometown. Why did she say that?"

"Aigo, she could have meant anything! Maybe she wanted you to visit your grandfather's grave, or your grandmother's."

"How about Fathers? Where is he buried?"

Eemo became silent. I didn't question her further. As much as I blamed both of them, I knew this was painful for her, too. Besides, I didn't need to hear more. Her silence was the confirmation I needed.

Yesterday morning, I booked a plane ticket to Pusan, Korea.

The last time I was there was when I was five. I remember very little about the entire trip. In fact, the only thing I can recall is the airport. Mom had made such a fuss about how I looked when we got off the plane. She made sure my hair was combed and my dress wasn't crumpled. I wondered why she did that. I wondered why she told me to ask that nice man in a suit where the telephone was. I saw that his hair was shiny and that he had double-slit eyelids. I wondered why he patted my hair and stroke my face before letting me return to Mom. I wondered why Mom walked to the

door more quickly when I returned from the man and didn't answer me when I asked her about the telephone. I wondered a lot of things. But I was either too young or too self-obsessed to ask. Now, I hold in my hand the photo of the man. In it he is much younger and he doesn't have the shiny hair, but he has the same creases over his eyelids. Just like me.
I place the letter, the photo and the plane ticket in my carry-on bag in preparation for my flight tomorrow and walk into Mom's room. I sit before the wooden dresser and look at myself in the mirror. It still reflects the twenty-five-year-old child. I still have the creases over my eyes. But this time, somehow, the image of Mom lingers in the dark shine of my pupils.

That night, I dream that I fly up to the sky. The moon is full, silver and smiling. I reach out and embrace it, and feel the silent ripples of the swallowed tears in my arms. Then, the moon bursts, and the tears flow out all around me, through my fingers, through my hair. And I hear Mom's laughter, loud and clear like the breaking of glass.

*Also published in Variety Crossing 3.*

# Midnight Whisky Party

Kee-Young Kang

Thinking it wouldn't do after circling around once in a big circle, Jung and I picked a spot. We happened to come upon a pond so we sat on the stones placed for decoration. The scenery was more beautiful than we could have hoped for. We could hear the sound of the water from the pond trickling down the gully. The grass of the golf course shone, wavering under the moonlight like a hill on a green field. The clusters of trees made the forest look darker.

"Care for a drink? I brought some."

I took out a 500 cc bottle of whiskey from my bag. It was the whiskey I had brought so that I could drink a glass or two on the way home. Usually I was unable to sleep deeply on the trip because of the worms that appeared on the back of my eyelids whenever I closed my eyes.

"Sure. I was just thinking it'd be nice to have some."

Jung was not a man for formalities. Without any hesitation, he gulped down a whole glass then straight away poured me some in return in the same glass.

"Strong, this whiskey..."

I remembered the time when I first immigrated to Paraguay. In the suffocating 40°C heat, often were the times when I drank because everything seemed depressing. Beer was too watery for someone used to soju, but whiskey was too strong—even this reality was depressing.

It has only been 6 months since Jung came to Canada, he said.
The alcohol went down smoothly after talking about each others' personal lives. With no ice, the lukewarm whiskey was stronger but the kim-bap was perfect as an appetizer.

"This is nothing. Some days, I had to work hanging off a rope."
Jung said he had worked as a welder in Korea. Since I only had school and café stories and Jung, construction site and bar room stories, we had no commonalities. But that was actually more entertaining when killing time. Jung lost his parents and siblings and became an orphan when he was six years old. Perhaps becoming a young orphan was a blessing-in-disguise because surprisingly, he said he never yearned for the love of his biological parents. He calmly told the story as if not his own. A devoted Catholic, his eldest uncle wished Jung to become a priest, but it was not part of his destiny as there was no student recruitment that year.

"We'll invite you after we get settled down so fulfill your army duties first."

This was the promise that his uncle had made when immigrating to Argentina. The person well-known for having six strong, healthy sons called "Jung's six brothers" in Buenos Aires was Jung's uncle. After having settled down, this time, his sons immigrated to Canada one by one. Because of the size of the big family, it took many years so Jung's immigration was pushed back. After finishing his army service term that he didn't even have to serve, Jung trained to become a welder since it was too boring to just blindly wait for the immigration. Time passed and he became a first-class technician, yet there was no news. All the while, Canada's immigration doors were closing in.

"Family is unbearably oppressive after having wandered around my whole life. I feel uncomfortable around my wife. She feels like a stranger to me. So when I get away with the excuse of catching worms for money, I feel that I can breathe."

This was the reason that Jung needlessly volunteered to catch worms for pay. Having married late, the Jung couple was a newlywed couple of just 4 months. He said that he had never lived in one place calling it his home for more than 3 months.

We had become old friends by the time the bottle was emptied. We decided to play hooky for the day and called it quits. Others must have had the same thought as we had for they had already quit and were waiting for the rest to come out. But there was no one who had totally wasted the day like we had. When we left at dawn even before the sun rose, we were excited like students returning home after having only completed morning classes.

"They say the weather tomorrow will be nice."

Manager Gu always insisted that it was "tomorrow" although strictly speaking, we returned home at dawn and left again the same night. Manager Gu repeated several times on the way home, "The weather is nice tomorrow."

*Translated by Hyeamin Yoon. Also published in Variety Crossing 7.*

# The Warm Echo of the Karma

JONG HAG LEE

Chul-min Kang had finished lunch with his wife and was enjoying a cup of coffee with watching snowflakes fall when he received a phone call. His daughter, Suzanne, had just been in a car accident.

The collision had taken place near Southgate at about 1:30. Days of snow had made the roads slick with ice. Suzanne had been waiting for the light to turn green when the car behind her slid into her bumper and pushed her car into an old man hobbling across the intersection. When Chul-min arrived at the scene, the accident had already been cleaned up. The car which rear-ended Suzanne's had been towed away and the old man was being carried to an ambulance.

Suzanne had been waiting for Chul-min on the sidewalk so they could go to the hospital together. In spite of the accident, she took the wheel, saving her aged father from driving the slick roads. As she drove, she explained to him what had happened.

"Daddy, the elderly man wasn't badly injured. I think he sprained his ankle or something when he fell – the roads are quite slippery. I know the accident wasn't my fault but I think it's better if I visit him since it was my car that hit him, don't you think?"

"Of course, Suzanne, it is a very good idea."

"The man is Chinese and he doesn't speak English. I was told he's here visiting his son. The ambulance workers have contacted him."

It wasn't difficult to find the old man in the Emergency Room. When Susanne and Chul-min arrived, he had already received some first aid and his right ankle was wrapped in a pressure bandage. His son was standing next to the bed. "They said the injury's not serious," he told them.

The old man looked to be in his late 70's. He was rather small and skinny but otherwise appeared quite healthy. He saw Suzanne and greeted her with his eyes. Suzanne apologized to him and asked, in English, how bad the injury was. His son interpreted as the old man smiled to let her know everything was going to be all right.

Suzanne introduced her father to the two men. Chul-min bowed, and as he approached the old man, he abruptly stopped. His eyes landed on the large scar in the middle of the old man's exposed right thigh. He felt Chul-min's gaze and stroked the scar.

"This is a bullet wound from the Korean War in 1952," he explained in Chinese.

Chul-min's eyes widened as he heard the son's translation. "Were you part of the Chinese Communist forces during the War?" he asked.

"Yes, I was. I fought in the Hwachon Battle."

"I … I am Korean. I also fought in Hwachon, Kyonggi as a young soldier."

The old man raised himself and abruptly grasped Chul-min's hands. "Ah, it's really nice to meet you," he said in Korean, though rather poorly.

He continued without giving Chul-min a chance to react. "I can speak and understand a bit of the language because my mother is from Korea."

This time it was Chul-min who grasped and shook the hands of the old man. They didn't need a translator any more. "You mentioned that you participated in the Hwachon Battle. Can you tell me more about it?" He pulled a chair closer to the bed and sat down, leaning in. The old man smiled and began telling his story.

"Even though it has been more than fifty years, I can remember it as if it was only yesterday," he began, "because I as almost killed that night."

"It was drizzling rain and there was a furious exchange of fire between our unit and the Koreans. As Platoon Commander I was in front, when suddenly I felt a sharp pain in my right leg. I fell. I had been shot in my thigh and I realized that there was no one who could help me. I had to take care of the wound myself. Eventually, the gunfire ended, and later when morning broke, I was finally able to check on my platoon. More than half had died in the battle. We had gone too far forward that night and had detached ourselves from the rest of the troops. We gathered ourselves and started to..."

"Wait, I am sorry but I must interrupt... tell me more about getting shot. How could you move around?"

As the old man gathered his thoughts to relate the details of that night, his eyes narrowed as he looked at Chul-min. A smile grew on his face as he shouted, "You were one of the Korean prisoners we took!"

Chul-min's memories of the war were as clear as the old man's. "Yes, I am."

The two embraced, hugging each other tightly and patting backs in honest joy. The enemies of a half century ago were like best friends now, grateful at this chance meeting a half world away.

That night, during the battle, the Chinese platoon had come across and captured two Korean soldiers lost in the dark. When the gunfire finally ended and the Chinese went searching for the rest of their troops, the two captives were forced to carry the Platoon Commander on a stretcher.

After setting up camp in the woods that early morning, a fighter plane appeared overhead, scattering the Chinese troops. Fearing American aircraft more than the King of Hell himself sent the Chinese looking for shelter from the enemy above.

The appearance of the fighter left the Platoon Leader alone with the two Korean soldiers behind some rocks. Some more planes appeared and circled, like eagles looking for prey. The wounded man looked at the captives lying curled up next to him and firmly whispered, "Run!"

"Run, now. Run! Now!" The words the leader shouted out were Korean. Stunned disbelief quickly turned to action as the two crawled to an embankment and rolled down towards a creek. The foliage and the confused panic brought on from the skies above created their escape.

Chul-min's fifty-year-old question, buried deep in his heart, was finally given the opportunity to be asked aloud. "Why did you spare us? Why did you let us escape from certain death? Tell me that one thing that's bothered me all these years."

The old man's answer was surprisingly simple. "The war was meaningless to me. I had no business there. Korea was my mother's homeland and I had no reason to fight against you."

There was no ideology. No grudge. No hostility. There was nothing between the platoon leader from the invading army and the Korean soldiers who fought against them to protect their homeland.

And today, more than fifty years later, the warm echo of karma was helping melt the Canadian snow.

*Translated by Hana Kim. Revised by Eugene Huh. Also published in Variety Crossing 6.*

# Non-Fiction

## "I was wrong to assume that the proclivities of one culture could be superimposed on another."

DAVID MACFARLANE

It's a downtown corner store, much like other.

The filmmaker, Paul Saltzman, buys the occasional lottery ticket there and it was Paul, a congenial and friendly fellow, who met Mr. and Mrs. Huh. Paul told Val Ross, who works for this newspaper, about the Baek-Ji Literary Club and about the collection of Korean-Canadian poetry that Mr. Huh had decided to publish. Publishing poetry seemed an unusual and interesting thing for a corner-store proprietor to be doing. And it was Val who called to tell me.

"Mr. who?" I asked.

"That's right," said Val.

Which, to make a long story short, was how my wife and I ended up sitting in rush-hour traffic, on our way to a Korean restaurant in a shopping mall in the northern reaches of Toronto. If you lie and work in downtown Toronto, it's easy to forget just how big a city it is. Just as, if you live and work in one culture, it's easy to forget how many other have been layered over this same sprawling geographic area. A big city is always bigger than most of its residents imagine. There are always more nationalities and races and religions and customs than most Torontonians ever guess—just as, so my wife and I were beginning to realize, there are always more stuck cars between wherever you are and wherever you want to be going.

We are going to be late because I had made the big mistake of forgetting how big Toronto is. In fact, as I try to guess how many lengths of immobile cars there could possibly be between Eglinton and Steeles, I began to wonder whether we would arrive at all.

We had been invited by Mr. Huh to attend the launch of the first edition of Forum-21, a Korean-Canadian literary journal that Mr. Huh and a few of his friends had worked hard to publish. Mr. Huh, a charming and energetic man, had thrown his heart and soul into the project.

"Very hard work," he said, conveying to me in those three words that as someone who had been given no easy route to success in his chosen country, he knew what he was talking about when it came to hard work. Forum-21, he believed, would prove to be a valuable contribution to Toronto's Korean community – a community that is now 60,000 strong. He hoped that many editions of the journal would follow the publication of the first.

Mr. Huh's invitation to us to join him in celebrating the publication of Forum-21 had been extended with a gracious solemnity. This was clearly an important event. So I phoned the restaurant from the car to apologize and to let him know that we were on our way. By then I'd told enough people about Mr. Huh to be reasonably certain how the first par the call to the restaurant would go.

"Could I speak to Mr. Huh?"

"Mr. who?"

"That's right."

Eventually, Mr. Huh was called to the phone. He said not to worry. He said it was no problem. Then he said precisely what I was hoping he wouldn't say: that everyone would wait until we arrived before anything began. Which was why my wife and I ended up running across a parking lot of a shopping mall, 45 minutes late for the Baek-Ji Literary Club's celebration dinner.

A book launch and poetry reading conjure certain images for me – none of which were fulfilled by the roomful of quiet, well-dressed people who were patiently awaiting our tardy arrival. No smoky bar. No plastic wine glasses. No literary gossip or squabbles. In fact, at first blush, the gathering looked more like the meeting of a Korean business association than a gathering of poets.

And this, as it turned out, was the biggest error I had made about the evening. I'd been wrong about how big the city is and I was wrong to assume that proclivities of one culture could be superimposed on another. The culture to which I belong, for instance, is quite adept at separating "artistic" things from everything else. We keep art in the art department. We keep poetry in the poetry section.

But this was a poetry reading. It was also, for the most part, a gathering of Korean businessmen and women – a group of conservative-looking, soft-spoken, friendly people who, apparently, saw nothing strange or peripheral or bohemian about spending several hours reading their poetry to one another. One by one the participants stood and read what were clearly heartfelt compositions to an attentive audience. Everybody clapped. Poetry, for these people, was a perfectly reasonable thing to be doing on a Friday evening.

Which, I couldn't help but think as we drove back home, is more than I can say for the rest of us.

*This article appeared in the Globe and Mail on December 6th, 1999. Also published in Variety Crossing 2.*

# Raising Bilingual Children

ELIZABETH COELHO
*Ontario Instititute for Studies Education, University of Toronto*

Did you that you can help your children future by continuing to use your own language in the home? Many studies in Canada and the US have shown that children who start learning English when they begin to school are not at a disadvantage – as long as they maintain and continue to develop in their first language. In fact, children who are equally skilled in two or more language have some definite advantages! This is the reason that many English speaking parents send their children to French Immersion school.

Here are some reasons for helping your children to continue to develop in your home language helping.

* Maintain your heritage language in the home helps families maintain good communication and close family ties.
* Their first language can be an important source of pride and identity for children who are living in two cultures.
* Children who can think and work more in then work one language are often more mentally flexible than children who use only one language.
* Children who have a strong foundation in their own language and who continue to develop at an age-appropriate level in that language will learn English better than children who stop developing in their language when they enter an English-language school environment.
* It takes at least five years for children to learn English sufficiently well to be able to do the kind of thinking, problem solving, reading and writing that they have to do in school. Therefore it is to their advantage if they can continue to think and solve problems in their first language, at least until English catches up.
* Bilingual children are often very good language learners when it comes to learning French or any other language at school.
* People who are fully bilingual may have more opportunities for employment.

How can you help your child to become bilingual?

Don't worry about speaking English at home. You can help your child more by providing a good model of your own language! Your child will be exposed to plenty of English at school, in the community, on TV, etc. Unless you are completely bilingual, concentrate on making sure that your child is exposed to many examples of your won language, both formal and informal.

* Talk to your child in your first language. For example, with young children, maintain a running commentary on what you are both doing. Tell stories, sing or play songs to your child, share proverbs, and recite poems. With children of all ages, make sure to talk often: tell them about your day, ask them about their day, discuss something in the news, and so on.

* Read to, and with, your child in your first language.

* Read a community language newspaper, watches TV shows in your language, and rent videos.

* Take your child with you to community events where they may hear your language spoken in more formal settings.

Talk with your child's teacher about your wish to raise a bilingual child, and give a copy of this article to the teacher.
Encourage your child to develop some school projects and assignment in two languages. For example: labeling a picture in languages, creating a bilingual picture book, or writing first drafts and outlines in the first language.

Volunteer to help in your child's school: maybe you can help a child who is just beginning to learn English. In this way you can not only help the child understand what's going on, but also be an example to all the children and teachers of the advantages of knowing more than one language.

Enroll your child in Heritage Language class, and visit the class to show support for the teacher. Sometime children are naturally reluctant to attend Heritage classes that are held on weekends: they would rather be out playing or socializing with their friends. Speak to the school principal about including heritage language classes during the school day. Did you know that Ontario secondary schools may offer credit course in any language as long as there are sufficient students to make up a class? Unfortunately, many language departments do not think of languages other than French, Italian, or Spanish – so it important to speak up on behalf of your community and request courses in your language.

*Also published in Variety Crossing 4.*

# Where there is a will, there is a way

Dae-Tong Huh

New connections and new encounters are happy occasions. They form the bridge of understanding, which gives birth to fresh emotions and exaltation. Even using the most high tech of computers, the beauty and depth of emotional connections between friends, neighbours and spouses are incalculable. Before me dance and sing the joys of new friendships.

This spring and summer had been hectic and exhausting for me, mentally and physically. We had no funds whatsoever, and we were attempting to publish our literary magazine "Variety Crossing" through private donations. Before us lay the unanticipated hardship of door to door soliciting. Having no previous experience of this type, and this being a multicultural society, planning such an ambitious project brought fear of becoming a mockery. I thought to myself, if I was hungry, I would work for a minimum wage, and if that didn't work, I would resort to begging. Despite my confidence, in reality I was afraid of unpredictable encounters and difficult questions that I would face. Even when I was determined to withstand all forms of humiliation, my quick temper and my pride had me in conflict for many days and nights.

One morning as I was deep in anxiety, my friend Paul came to see me. He is the kind of person who can comfort you with just his smile. "How are you, Dae-Tong?" his deep baritone voice asked as he looked into my face. I cut to the chase: "I need funds for a publication." I asked for his help. Despite my unexpected request, he smiled and answered, "How much do you want?" His friendly response surprised me and made me happy. I told him. He replied, "I will let you know," and left the store.

After our little meeting, I felt uneasy for several days. I felt as though I had made a mistake that could jeopardize our friendship. Then Paul phoned me. He always speaks to me in the calm and open tone that only exists between close friends. "What do you think this?" he asked as he mentioned an amount. I was ecstatic. These few words gave me an incredible boost of energy. They were proof that my attempt at imitating *"Kim Sat Kat's begging" was possible. Thus, I began preparing the letters to initiate the process of seeking donations. However, I was still hindered by a feeling of "what-if?".

After a few days, I thought it would be of help to hear my friend David's opinion. He's a man with a lot of experience in publishing. I called him and said "I would like to have lunch with you tomorrow to discuss what I have in mind." David agreed readily.

That night I couldn't sleep. As the prospect of begging for donations became more and more uncertain, I couldn't get anything done. Like the anxiety a captain feels heading out on a voyage into the unknown, I felt the same apprehension overwhelming me in a giant wave. I was unsure whether I could stand the storm, let alone how I would maneuver the ship.

The next day, David and I met at a Korean restaurant on Bloor Street. As we ate fresh kimbap and hot miso soup, I began: "I'm so worried. Begging for money like this is a first for me. I don't know if it's going to be possible. I wish for your opinion."

He was listening intently. I showed him the letter that I was going to use to obtain donations. After carefully reading it, he said, "It is a good idea, but how much money do you expect to acquire through donations?" I didn't have an answer for him. The only thing I could mention was the cheque I had received from Paul. After listening, he comforted and encouraged me by saying, "I will look into it." This helped me gain the confidence to pursue the project further.

However, when it came down to it, words stayed on the tip of my tongue, refusing to come out as I ventured into the world of possible donors. My pride had sealed my mouth shut. My objective was a dream that couldn't move forward without meeting new people and talking to them. I had to shed myself of my ego – how Mother Nature intended me to be. I called Jerry, a friend who works at the fruit and vegetable market, and asked for his opinion. "I need money to publish a book. Would you support for me?" He answered, "I will think about that." Thus I began my painstaking process of establishing connections through patience and long waits.

It was obvious that some people disapproved of what I was doing. But I had gone too far to turn back now. I had dreams of being caught in a trap. I moaned in my sleep. One day, as I returned to the store from another heart-breaking disappointment, harsh words tore me apart. My patience was running short. My breathing became shallow and painful. I suddenly felt that I had to grab my bag and drive somewhere to comfort my broken heart and prevent myself from acting rashly.

After three hours, I arrived at Percy Lake, just north of Haliburton. I sat dipping my feet into the unpolluted crystal-clear lake. Behind me, oak trees were gathering sunshine to set the summer ablaze, and the sun's rays shining down on the valley were warming the water. The gentle touch of a summer breeze, the quiet gestures of trees enveloped me like a folding screen; all of these things calmed my heart. I felt a sense of peace. It was a gift from my encounter with nature. I looked up at the feathery blue sky. It had opened up its heart. Everything was naked before me. The encounter healed my wounds. Fresh energy rippled in my heart like the peaceful lake water.

After a few days, David dropped by at the store. While I talked to him about collecting donations, he handed over a cheque. My heart was moved, and I said, "I can't accept your money." What I needed from him was his help as an established writer, but here he was, offering me a heartfelt donation, which was more than I asked for. Tears lingered in my eyes. I had received a gift of warmth that couldn't be expressed in words. Like spring that marches forth and melts the winter, like the pulse of summer that begins the season, a powerful wave rushed over me. It gave me strength that no one or no thing could take away. It was as though clouds disappeared to reveal the blue sky. The light of hope burned away the darkness, like the silent lustre of stars at night. "I'll go out to the front lines!" I held my Torch and walked forth into the rain and the waves.

To voyage is to overcome storms. During a stroll through my own storm, I met generous hands of different races, and their love and support filled the donation basket. The sincerity of kind farmers, the encouragement of people of many levels of society, and the support of Korean-Canadians all helped to form "the basket of new encounters". The magazine was an unborn child, and this basket nurtured the womb in which this child of our effort was conceived and grew.

In this way, I had collected the publishing funds needed in a month and a half. Through the support of over 50 individuals of various ethnicity, my hardships quickly transformed into the joy of forming new friendships. I met and spoke with many people at places such as the Ontario Food Terminal, restaurants, the street and even barber shops. From these encounters, I had the chance to observe and experience multiculturalism first hand. It was a strenuous voyage, but when I look back on it now, it was the first time in 35 years of living as a foreigner that I truly experienced the multi-cultural society as a participant. I actually lived the saying, "Where there is a will, there is a way". I had gained so much and learned even more. The fact that the accumulated donations could cover the entire cost of the publication was an astounding gift for myself and for our group.

So, this is how, after 3 or 4 months, the magazine "Variety Crossing" was born. The names of those who supported us remain at the back of the book (Second Edition) in their original handwriting. After paying the fees, the funds have hit rock bottom once again. However, as I thank each and everyone of those who supported us, I promise myself that I will work diligently for the development of the multi-cultural society for 1.5 and second generation Korean-Canadians.

I went out to our back yard to cut the overgrown grass, neglected over the months of my preoccupation with the magazine. The summer heat, rain and the wind had nurtured the grass into entangled hippie hair. The lawn mower groaned under the strain and beads of sweat trickled down my forehead. The cry of the mower evoked images of the friendly encounters, the harsh words, and the pains and joys of conversation. My gratitude became a dove and flew up to the sky, ever so lightly and ever so high.

*Translated by Hyeamin Yoon & Helen Kang.*

**Kim Sat Kat was a sage who, to escape the corrupted world, set out and wandered aimlessly, living the life of an ascetic. He begged for food and provisions in order to survive. Hence, the expression here implies extreme toil.*

# Interview

## The Unfinished War

INTERVIEW WITH BRIAN MCKENNA: FRIDAY, NOVEMBER 7TH, 2003

Dae-Tong Huh (DTH)
Brian McKenna (B McK)

**DTH:**

The young generation living in Canada and the States — they don't know what the real story is in Korea, but when they watch the documentary, there will be something that touches them. It will show them what war is. And was. I'm so happy and proud to meet you and discuss this film with you

**B McK:**

Thank you so much. That's a great compliment you pay me.
It is very easy for a Canadian filmmaker to go somewhere else in the world, and we decided that we weren't just going to tell the story of Canadians fighting in Korea, we were going to tell the story of a war that is still going on, and that was a big challenge. And we wanted to be very respectful of an ancient country but at the same time try and make sense of this terrible war. And I think that all of us who looked at this war could not believe how terrible it was. It's now called the Forgotten War, but it was almost the Third World War! And in terms of the casualties, at least a million people — ordinary civilians — in South Korea, annihilated. 2.5 million people in North Korea killed, never mind all of the soldiers who died on both sides: Korean soldiers, and then all the Western soldiers, and all the Chinese soldiers. It's a staggering, staggering war, and how it could be called a Forgotten war is beyond belief if you've studied it or looked at it closely

**DTH:**

If you don't have experience in war, the mere word is not enough to describe it. The war was long ago, but I still feel the effects in my heart. I think that's why we began Variety Crossings, our journal of multicultural poetry and prose. My poetry helps me release these feelings that have been kept inside for all these years. I also felt very touched because your film also reminded me of these feelings as I watched and remembered this war. Most of your past work focuses on Canadian History: Pierre Trudeau, Native Canadians, the War of 1812. What inspired you to tell the story of the Korean War?

**B McK:**

It's true that much of my work is focused on the history of Canada – very often the hidden history of Canada. But in the last five or ten years, I've been branching out and looking wider. For example, when we did the story of the First Nation leaders – the Chiefs – we didn't just focus on the ones who happened to be in what may have been called Canada or the United States. We focused on the best leaders in North America. We told their stories regardless of what nationality.

I think I was inspired by working with (former Canadian Prime Minister) Pierre Trudeau, because I worked with him for almost two years making the film about him and his memoirs of political life. He always called himself a citizen of the world. So I would like to see myself not only as a fierce Canadian, but also as a citizen of the world. And as a citizen of the world, I have a responsibility as a filmmaker to tell stories and recount history and, I believe, to dig into hidden history, to bring stories like this out, not just for Canadians but for the international community.

**DTH:**

You use an interesting technique of presenting quotes – from General MacArthur and journalist Marguerite Higgens among others – by having actors speak their words in reenactment. Why did you choose this method rather than simply reading their thoughts through a voiceover?

**B McK:**

Well, in terms of just reading, I'm not giving a college lecture. I'm a filmmaker. In the United States, there's a technique of showing a picture of a person and having an actor read the text under the picture. I find those films put me to sleep after a while. It's not a film; it's a beautiful, illustrated slide lecture. So when I make a film, I throw my heart and soul into it, my passion into it. Whatever I can find to help me to tell my story. If it's poetry, if it's the art, if it's the stock footage taken by the different armies – the North Korean, the South Korean, the Chinese, the Canadian, American army, feature films, Chinese feature films, American feature films, American documentary films – whatever material I can find to use, I put it all into the documentary.

The words of MacArthur, the words of Yu Chun Do, the words of the young Canadian soldiers, it's very important to me. I want to capture the spirit of what it was like when these soldiers were 20 or 22, so that's one of the principle reasons we use the actors. But we are very, very careful with the actors we chose. He or she may not look like the person perfectly, but there's something about their spirit that captures the essence.

**DTH:**

The casting is so well done — the first time I watched this, I could not tell whether it was real or whether this was acting — the connections were done so naturally. So how long were you in Korea for this film?

**B McK:**

The actual time in Korea was very concentrated. So much of the work we do is in the preparation. We spent a year researching and then six months preparing the filming, so when we arrived, first in North Korea – and it was very unusual to be invited to come to North Korea – we knew exactly what we needed to get. And when we went to South Korea, same thing: we have to go to the DMZ (Demilitarized Zone), we have to talk to certain people.

**DTH:**
Now, you mentioned a little bit about the war. War is never pleasant, but what, in your opinion, made this conflict especially ugly?

**B McK:**
Racism.
It was very clear to us when we started working with the veteran Canadian and American soldiers that all Koreans – Communist, fascist Koreans, friendly Koreans – all Koreans were called 'gooks'. This is a racist epithet that was used to describe all Korean people, and it was very much a product of the time.

If you see someone not as a person, but as a 'gook' then it's much easier to kill them. It's much easier to pour napalm over them. It's much easier to torture them. It's much easier to use them as cannon fodder. So, clearly, this is a very, very crucial component of why the Korean people had to suffer the devastating casualties.
It was because of racism.

**DTH:**
You interviewed many people whose lives were changed by the war. Men who fought there, people who were rescued, eyewitnesses to the conflict. Was there anything common among them?

**B McK:**
The common human traits of heroism. And cowardice sometimes. Grief at losing family, friends. Courage in the face of terrible, terrible things happening. Patience, optimism – the same feelings that I have. We're all human, and nothing brings it home more than war. People react the same way.

**DTH:**

During this project, you were actually allowed to enter North Korea and meet with some of the people. How were you able to do that?

**B McK:**

It was principally because of James Endicott's reputation in the 1950's and his son Stephen's work when he wrote this very important book on the use of biological warfare during the Korean War. It was coincidental that at the same time we began working on this film, Stephen Endicott got a call from the North Koreans asking, 'Would you like to come?' He said, 'Well, I'm working on this film with these filmmakers.' So they checked us out, and I guess they decided that we'd at least try and report their story fairly, without agreeing with anything they represent. So they invited us to come with Stephen Endicott, and that's how we ended up in North Korea.

**DTH:**

Usually, when ordinary people visit North Korea, they would have the Secret Police follow them. Did you see anything like this?

**B McK:**

Well, no, we had three people assigned to stay with us – in English, we call them 'Minders' – they were controlling us. We would put the camera down and they would say "Why are you filming? What are you filming?" And if you start filming people, and the people see you – I think people are punished if they're caught being filmed or photographed by a Western camera crew.

But after a while, we explained to them that if we're going to tell the story of North Korea during the war, we've got to film ordinary people now. So they let us. Every day that passed, they let us film more and more. But still, it was very controlled. We went outside of Pyongyang, but we didn't go far.

**DTH:**

So what were your feelings about being there, and did you ever feel like you were in danger?

**B McK:**

We never felt we were in danger. First of all, coming into North Korea – into Pyongyang – it's a strange experience. This is the international airport, Like Pearson (International Airport in Toronto), but it has fewer flights than Tuktuyuktuk in the Northwest Territories. It has two flights a week to Beijing, and it's a big deal. Guys in uniforms come out and customs are set up twice a week. That's the international airport. Talk about isolation.

When we arrived, they were very polite and very helpful, but there would be three North Koreans who were going to stay with us all the time. One of them was sleeping in the same hotel, on the same floor all the time.

They were explaining and justifying, arguing – it was an engaging intellectual experience. They were intelligent, they could be very funny, but not about North Korean politics. Or their dear, great leader.

At one point I raised the question, "I don't really understand how, in a socialist communist country, that state power can pass from a father to a son. It sounds feudal to me." And our host Mr. Pak, who represented the Democratic Lawyers Association, said "How dare you!"

He made it clear to me that I was insulting his country, insulting his leader and he said to me, "Kim Jong Il is the leader of our country, not because he was the son of Kim Il Sung, but because he is the most brilliant, talented politician in the country, someone whose natural leadership allowed him to be chosen for the job as leader of North Korea. It is a coincidence that he is the son of Kim Il Sung." And I sat there waiting for the joke. But it was no joke

**DTH:**

If you could talk to the leaders of the North Koreans...

**B McK:**
As a filmmaker, all I can say is I'd like to interview Kim Jong Il. I'd like the world to meet him. I'm sure they'd be surprised.

**DTH:**
Did you arrange to see him?

**B McK:**
We asked, but no Western filmmaker or journalist, no matter how sympathetic they were to the North has ever been allowed to interview Kim Jung Il. And we were not sympathetic.

**DTH:**
What was the general feeling about the standoff among the North Koreans, and how much do they understand about how the world sees them?

**B McK:**
They have no idea.
It's terrifying how isolated they are. How the regime has been able to maintain this Orwellian control. They block off all television signals, almost all radio signals, all newspapers, all magazines, all Internet. This is a country that's frozen in time. Sometimes you feel it's 50 years ago, sometimes you feel it's 5000 years ago.

It is very sad, the degree of isolation. And people were that isolated. And fearful to make mistakes. But what was clear from everyone we talked to in Korea – North Korea, South Korea – everyone wants unification. This is one country. Just like Germany was one country. In Germany, eventually the forces brought it back together again. And some day, North Korea and South Korea are going to come back together again. Everyone's got their own plan, but all the plans mean the same thing: Unification.

**DTH:**

Yes, I hope some day.

**B McK:**

And people – both sides – don't want war. And the North, they said "we had so many tears, so much blood. We don't want another war. We will do anything. But we need help."

The war is still on. That's not clear to most people. It's the same war. It's not finished. There was no peace treaty. It's the same war, the same issues, and it's probably the most dangerous place in the world right now.

**DTH:**

What do you hope this documentary does for viewers?

**B McK:**

Back in the 1960's, as a student, we always had a saying that we used, it became our mantra: "Information is power. Power to the people." So people should know what happened.

We have to try and strip away the lies; strip away the propaganda; strip away the ideology and say "here is the story that as far as we know, is true in terms of what happened." So it's very important for me to tell the truth; I was always taught to tell the truth. In filmmaking, it's central to who I am and what I do.

What I see may be uncomfortable to report it for someone, it may be uncomfortable for me to report it – sometimes the communists weren't all bad, sometimes the fascists did good work – but I must report the truth. I can't say, well you know, I'm supporting the South or I'm supporting the North – my job is to bear witness to the truth.

So if I've informed Canadians and anyone else around the world who sees the documentary about the situation in Korea and make them more sympathetic to what's happening, make them more understanding, make them understand that there's so much at stake, that the world can go into another war because of Korea – and we must not let that happen – this is all very important to me.

We have two reasons for trying to understand the Korean War. One, because in 1950, we sent soldiers to fight and die – that's a good reason. There's another very powerful reason: so many people from Korea have come to Canada and are now Canadians, so their stories are a part of our history. And so to tell our history, we have to tell their stories too. We're bound together and we must acknowledge that.

*This interview is a shortened transcript of the exclusive, 1-hour interview by Korean-Canadian Literary Forum-21 publisher, Dae-Tong Huh of filmmaker, Brian McKenna about his documentary "The Unfinished War" (About the June 25, 1950 Korean War) on November 10-13, 2003 at TV Ontario Studio. His documentary was shown over four days.*

*Transcript by Jaak Raun. Korean translation by Dae-Tong Huh. Also published in Variety Crossing 6.*

# Biography

Barnes, Lilly

Born in Russia, Lilly studied at the University of Toronto and the University of Vienna, and worked for many years as an arts journalist and scriptwriter for CBC Radio and Television. Among her recent works is the novel Invisible Border.

Bhargava, Ashok

Ashok Bhargava is a Vancouver based poet whose poetry reflects his interest in humanity, history, travel, Internet technology and love without borders. His poetry reveals the individuality of people and cultures by giving shape and form to feelings, emotions and sentiments. He holds a Masters degree in Economics. He is recipient of an "Ambassador Poet" award from the World Poetry Reading Series. His poetry has been published in various literary magazines and anthologies. He has been a featured poet on CFMQ 105 radio station. He was also featured at the Word on the Street and the Asian Heritage Month Festivals. He writes in English and Hindi. He is currently learning the Hangul language. Books authored by Ashok include: Mirror of Dreams (Keuyon Press, Seoul, South Korea), A Kernel of Truth (Rawhsi Publishing, Vancouver, BC), Skipping Stones (Virgo Publishing, Mississauga, Ontario), and Half Open Door (self published).

Brossard, Nicole

Montreal-based poet, novelist, and essayist. She has published eight novels and many books of poetry. Literary awards include Governor General award (1974, 1984), Le Grand Prix de Poesie de la Foundation les Forges (1989, 1999), Le Prix Athanase-David for a lifetime of literary achievement (1991), the Harbourfront Festival Prize. A member of L'Academie des Lettres du Quebec (1994). Nicole was recently shortlisted for the 2008 Griffin Poetry Prize.

Byun, Hae Myung

Member of the Korean PEN-Centre, Essayist and Secretary of the Korean Association of Essayists (Seoul, Korea).

Callaghan, Barry

Born in Toronto, Barry Callaghan has been a professor at York University since 1966. From 1966 to 1971, he was literary editor for Toronto Telegram; a producer and war correspondent for CBC's Public Affairs from 1968-71; a commentator on CTV network from 1976-1982 and is the founder and editor of Exile: A Literary Quarterly and Exile Editions.

Chao, Lien

Poet, anthologist and critic, Lien Chao was born in China in 1950 and came to Canada in 1984 to study Canadian literature. She eventually completed both M.A. and Ph.D. degrees at York University. Her Ph.D. dissertation is an examination of Chinese-Canadian literature and it formed the basis for her book of literary criticism Beyond Silence. Chao continues to live in Toronto.

Clarke, George Elliott

2001 Governor General's Award Winner for English Poetry for *Execution Poems*. He is a poet, playwright, literary critic, professor of English at the University of Toronto. He has also taught at Duke University. His awards include The Portia White Prize for Artistic Achievement, a Bellagio Center Fellowship, and the Outstanding Writer in Film and Television Award. He also received The Order of Canada.

Cosma, Flavia

Flavia Cosma was born in Romania. She has published poems in English and Romanian and has written, produced, and directed TV documentaries and children's plays. Recipient of the ALTA Richard Wilbur Prize for

Poetry in Translation for 47 Poems (1989; Translations by Dr. Don Wilson with the author) and the Canadian Scene National Award for the TV Documentary Romania A Country at the Crossroads (1991). Member of the Writer's Union of Canada, PEN International- Canada, the Canadian Ethnic Journalists and Writers.

D'ALFONSO, ANTONIO

Poet & publisher. Born in Montreal in 1953. He studied at Loyola College and Université de Montréal. In 1978, he founded Guernica Editions, where he edited over one hundred books by authors from around the world. An author himself, he has published a number of books in French and English.

DICKSON, ROBERT

As a poet, he has left his mark on the artistic landscape in both French and English — as cofounder of the poetry/music/performance group La Cuisine de la poésie, as actor, as lyricist, and asthe translator of several plays. He was awarded the Prix du Nouvel-Ontario (1998), the Prix du Centre de recherche en civilisation-française of the University of Ottawa(1999), the Governor General's Award, 2002, for his poem Humains paysages en temps de paix relative. He is professor of literature at Laurentian University in Sudbury.

DODA, CHRISTOPHER

Poet. His debut collection of poems, Among Ruins, published by Mansfield Press in 2001, was widely acclaimed by critics. Lives and writes in Toronto.

FETHERLING, GEORGE

Author and editor of over 50 books of poetry, fiction, essays, criticism, travel, and biography. Former literary editor of the Kingston Whig-Standard and the Toronto Star, former writer-in-residence at Queen's

University and the University of New Brunswick. His awards include D.Litt honoris causa, St. Mary's University; Harbourfront Festival Prize; shortlisted for Trillium Award for Travels By Night; and Asia-Pacific Foundation Fellow in China.

HARRY J. HUANG

Also known as Freeman J. Wong, Harry J. Huang is one of the world's leading authorities in Chinese-English literary translation. He is a college English professor, methodologist and bilingual writer. He has authored 130 English stories published in three collections, entitled Nothing Comes of Nothing, Morality, Eh?, and A Bride in Washington. He has published five English textbooks, including Essential College Writing Skills and Refining the Sentence as well as early childhood education how-to books, among others. He has translated into English more than 100 Chinese authors, stories, poems, as well as songs including the "National Anthem of the People's Republic of China." He has been teaching English in Seneca College since 1989, before which he had taught English and translation in Sun Yat-sen University for eight years. His books, essays and articles have been published in Canada, China, Britain, America, Brazil and Italy. He won a social research award (1989) and a literary award Sun Yat-sen Book Award (2005) for his English translation An Anthology of Chinese Short Short Stories.

HUH, EUGENE

Holds of an Engineering degree from University of Toronto. He lives in Vancouver where he writes poetry and prose. His other hobbies include graphic design, travel, and photography.

HUH, DAE-TONG

Born in Korea, landed in Canada in 1969. Poet, translator & publisher, president of the Korean-Canadian Literary Forum-21, Toronto. Member of the Korean PEN-Centre, Canadian Ethnic Journalists' & Writers' Club and The Writers' Union of Canada. He is the author of over thirty poems, stories and essays published in various anthologies, magazines and newspapers. His first book of selected poetry, More Waves, was published in 2004. He was appointed President of the Korean District PEN in Canada by the International Korean PEN Centre in 2006. He recently received a Translation Grant from the Daesan Foundation in Korea for Ripples due out in 2008. He recently translated Sang Kim's play, A Dream Called Laundry, into Korean. It is published by Minerva, a publishing house in Korea. He recently finished the translation of a selection of Korean Contemporary Poems. It will be published in Korea.

JEUNG, CHOONG MO
Poet and member of the Korean-Canadian Literary Forum-21, Korean Literature Association, Earth Literary Association, and the International Korean PEN Centre.

KANG, HELEN entered the PhD (Sociology) program in Fall 2005 after completing an MSc in social science and health from the University of Toronto and a BASc from McMaster University. Helen's research interests include cultural studies, visual studies, social studies of science and technology and critical pharmaceutical studies. Her dissertation examines the relationships among the pharmaceutical industry, the medical profession, and patient-consumers through a textual analysis of pharmaceutical advertising. Helen is working with Profs Cindy Patton, Dany Lacombe, and Zoë Druick.

KATO, MOLINARI
She was born in Alta Gracia, hills of Córdoba, Argentina. She holds a Master of Arts (Universidad Nacional de Córdoba). Poetess, narrator and translator. Published books include:

"Por boca de quién" (1972); "Miradas y peregrinaciones" (1982); "Noche de las cosas, mitad del mundo"; "Las simias" (1989); "Umbral" (1993); "Un jerónimo de duda" (1996), "Una hormiga/un halcón" (2004). She won several prices for her literary work and is invited to read in foreign countries. She lives in Buenos Aires.

Kim, Suji Kwock

2002 Walt Whitman Award Winner from the Academy of American Poets. She was shortlisted for the Griffin Poetry Prize for Notes from the Divided Country. She is an associate professor of English Literature at Drew University.

Ko, Un

Born in Kunsan (province of North Cholla) in 1933, Ko Un is the most controversial and the most prolific Korean writer alive. He has published well over a hundred volumes of poetry, fiction, essays, translations, and drama. Translations of his work have been published in several languages. He is an honorary member of the Griffin Trust.

L'Abbe, Sonnet

Born in Toronto. Her first book of poetry, A Strange Relief, was published by McClelland and Stewart in 2001. Her work also appears in Open Field: 30 Contemporary Canadian Poets, and in Red Silk: An Anthology of South Asian Canadian Women Poets. L'Abbe is the recipient of the Malahat Review Long Poem Prize and of the Bronwen Wallace Award for most promising writer under 35. She is currently completing her Ph. D. of English literature.

Lee, Jong Hag

Adviser of the Korean Literary Club of Edmonton. He is a member of the Korea Literature Association and the Korean Association of Novelists. His

Korean publications include short stories, Noon Mon Mal and novel, Tae Son among others.

LEE, WOO SIN

Poet and professor at Canada Christian College.

KIM, NHAM CHO

Nham Cho Kim debuted through The Yonhap Newspaper in 1948. As a poet, she published the following collections: Life, The Tree and Wind, Sentimental Period, and many other books of poetry. She won the May Literary Art Award and The Literature Award of Seoul City. Currently she is an Honorary Professor of Sookmyung Women's University, and a member of the Art Academy.

LEE, GIL-WON

Gil-Won Lee debuted through poetry literature. As a poet, he published Becoming of a tree of the once morning, Psalm Haeyiri, and many others works. He won the Cheonsangbyeong Poetry Award. Currently he is the Vice Director of The International Korean PEN Centre.

MACFARLANE, DAVID

David Macfarlane is the author of the novel, Summer Gone, short-listed for the 1999 Giller Prize and the co-winner of the Chapters/Books in Canada First Novel Award. His previous book, The Danger Tree, is a memoir of his Newfoundland relatives, centred largely on their experiences in the First World War. It won the Canadian Authors' Award for Non-fiction. Both books have been published internationally.

Macfarlane has also written short-stories and poetry, as well as articles for magazines and scripts for documentary film. He is the recipient of numerous Canadian National Magazine Awards.

His weekly column in The Globe and Mail won a National Newspaper

Award for critical writing in 1997 and was nominated again in 1998. He is currently working on a book on the marble quarries of Tuscany.

MARTIN, LINDA

Linda Martin McGregor is a First Nations writer, educator, conference presenter born and raised at Six Nations of the Grand River Territory in southern Ontario. She received an eagle feather in recognition of her contributions in raising the profile of Aboriginal people, culture and music as the producer and host of Rock 95's Spirit Wind.

MCGREGOR, MARION

Marion McGregor (Wassetekwe - Bright Place Woman) is a retired elementary school teacher and principal of Shawanasowe School in Whitefish River First Nation on Manitoulin Island. She is a recipient of a Lifetime Achievement Award from the Union of Ontario Indians and an eagle feather for her community service. Marion has assisted the Ojibwe Cultural Foundation with the translation of school curriculum into Ojibwe and is involved in translating children's speeches for Ojibwe speech contests.

MARIA PIA MARCHELLETTA

She studied both Italian and French literature and grammar at the University of Toronto. The Ontario Poetry Society, Canadian Authors Association, Vaughan Poet's Circle, The Association of Italian-Canadian Writers, Canadian Federation of Poets, Poetry Ireland, The Poetry Society, UK and Toastmasters International where she has shared her poetry.

Most recent publications include The Poet Band Company of Pennsylvania, The Ontario Poetry Society and the Canadian Federation of Poets. She is passionate about music, family and friends and especially travelling to Mexico. She is currently working on her first poetry book entitled, "Nocturnal Laments".

Michaels, Anne

Anne Michael's novel, Fugitive Pieces, was shortlisted for the Giller Prize and the Canadian Booksellers Association Author of the Year Award, and won the Trillium Prize, the Chapters/Books in Canada First Novel Award, The Beatrice and Martin Fischer Award, and England's prestigious Orange Prize. Her collections of poetry, The Weight of Oranges won the Commonwealth Prize for the Americas and Miner's Pond won the Canadian Authors Association Award and was shortlisted for the Governor General's Award and the Trillium Award.

Mikhail Park

Poet, artist and writer in Russia

Moon, Hyo-Chee

Chief Director of PEN International- Korea and Associate Professor at Juseong College. He has published 10 books of poetry and 3 books of essays. Recipient of Dongguk University Literature Award, PEN International Korea Literature Award, and various other poetry awards.

Park, Je-Chun

Je-Chun Park, debuted through the Modern Literature Award. As a poet, he published Chuang-tzu's poem and 12 other poetry collections. He received the Korean Poetry Association Award, Modern Literature Award. Currently he is the publisher of the Literature Academy.

Rivera, Patria

Patria Rivera was born and raised in the Philippines. She graduated from the University of the Philippines with a degree in journalism and continued her media studies in Australia and Germany. She now lives in Toronto, Ontario.

Rosenblatt, Joe

Governor General's Award Winner for Poetry for his selected poems (1962-1975), Top Soil and The 1986 B.C. Book Prize Winner for poetry for Poetry Hotel. He has published more than a dozen books of poetry and fiction. He has held writer-in-residence positions at Canadian universities and short term positions at the University of Rome and University of Bologna. He was the former President of The League of Canadian Poets. His artwork is showcased in the Rosenblatt Collection of Carleton University Art Gallery, Ottawa.

Saltzman, Paul

Emmy Award-winning Toronto-based film producer/director and prose writer. Lives in Toronto.

Siedlecki, Charles

He was born in Montreal in 1950 and makes his home in Toronto. He is an educator, writer and translator who has published his poems and film criticism in various journals. He is currently preparing a collection of his poems in book form.

Song, Kijo

Poet. He was a Professor at the Korean National Teachers' University. Currently, he is the honorary chairman of the Korean Literary Association.

Sward, Robert

Poet and prose writer. Born in Chicago, he has made a brilliant career as a professor at a number of American universities (Cornell, Iowa, Connecticut College). He teaches at the University of California.

Teleky, Richard

Richard Teleky teaches in the Humanities Division of York University. His books include The Paris Years of Rosie Kamin, received the Ribalow Prize (U.S.) for the best novel of 1999, a recent novel, Pack Up the Moon, and Hungarian Rhapsodies: Essays on Ethnicity, Identity and Culture.

Uppal, Priscila

Fiction writer and poet. Born in Ottawa and currently lives in Toronto. Author of two books of poetry, as well as selected poems and short stories in national and international magazines. She is Professor of Humanities at York University. Priscila was recently shortlisted for the 2007 Griffin Poetry Prize.

Viccari, Ben

President of the Canadian Ethnic Journalists' and Writers' Club. Ben Viccari is a Toronto writer, editor and television commentator.

Yevtushenko, Yevgeny

Born in Siberia, Russia, Yevtushenko is internationally acclaimed as Russia's most famous living poet. He has written essays and toured the world as a speaker, currently spending half of the year teaching at Tulsa University in Oklahoma.

Yoo, Kyung Whan

Born in the province of Hwanghae. Educated in Korea and Hawaii, he obtained his Ph. D. from Yonsei University in Seoul. Author of 14 books of poetry.

Yoon, Hyeamin

Translator and writer

Yoon, Hyung Bok

Poet, CSC University professor, and author of 15 books. Lives in Toronto.

Submissions: Variety Crossing reads short stories, essays and poetry from January 1st to May 1st. We are open to new and established writers.
All submissions can be e-mailed to:
dt_huh@yahoo.ca / varietycrossing@gmail.com
Please visit our web site for additional details:
http://www.varietycrossing.org